VANISHING VALLEJO

Random History Notes on a Colorful California Town

Brendan Riley

AMERICA
THROUGH TIME®
ADDING COLOR TO AMERICAN HISTORY

America Through Time is an imprint of Fonthill Media LLC
www.through-time.com
office@through-time.com

Published by Arcadia Publishing by arrangement with Fonthill Media
LLC
For all general information, please contact Arcadia Publishing:
Telephone: 843-853-2070
Fax: 843-853-0044
E-mail: sales@arcadiapublishing.com
For customer service and orders:
Toll-Free 1-888-313-2665

www.arcadiapublishing.com

First published 2022

ISBN 978-1-63499-421-7

Typeset in 10pt on 13pt Sabon
Printed and bound in England

Acknowledgments

In writing the columns included in this book, I reviewed many old stories and history columns that ran in years past in newspapers in Vallejo, other San Francisco Bay area cities, and elsewhere around the country. These accounts were not always complete. Thanks to internet search tools that were not available in the past, I was able to find more details and expand upon those earlier accounts.

My parents, Wyman and Marjorie Riley, both journalists and writers, years ago sparked my interest in writing and history, both by their writing and by stories they would tell at home. My father's history columns, which he wrote from 1957 to 1963 as managing editor of the *Vallejo Times-Herald*, provided me with many ideas for columns of my own. Other important resources included history books, columns, and articles written in years past by Arnold Lott, Ernie Wichels, Sue Lemmon, Dave Beronio, Lee Fountain, Frank Leach, Tom Lucy, and others.

Historian Jim Kern, former executive director of the Vallejo Naval and Historical Museum, gave me full access to the museum's research library, archives, and photo collections; most importantly, he shared his extensive knowledge of local history in discussing possible column topics. Museum staffer Mary Kuykendall searched through museum files and old newspapers whenever I was unable to get to the museum for information needed to write and illustrate columns.

Rick Mariani, professional photographer and president of the Vallejo Naval and Historical Museum's board of directors, assisted in preparing the photographs that illustrate many of the columns in this book.

Among those who encouraged me to write, shared ideas, and provided good advice were Paula McConnell, Carol Jensen, Sharon McGriff-Payne, Dennis Kelly, Jerry Bowen, Gary Cullen, Mel Orpilla, Joyce Giles, Barbara Davis, John Watson, Fred Sessler, and Mike Ioakimedes.

Many other Vallejoans assisted in the writing of these columns, some with their own memories dating to World War II and even earlier. Others, whose families have been in Vallejo for generations, shared stories that had been told to them by their parents and grandparents.

Maggie Tracey, my spouse, was my main source of encouragement. She read every word I wrote, with a good editor's eye and with high interest. I could not have completed this without her.

Contents

Introduction

The columns in this book represent a selection of the Solano Chronicles articles, focused on the history of Vallejo, Mare Island, and other areas of Solano County that I began writing in 2017. The column-writing began following the publishing of my book about Vallejo's infamous sailor district: *Lower Georgia Street: California's Forgotten Barbary Coast*. In the course of writing the book, I amassed a small mountain of notes, files, photos, and other materials that dealt with many other aspects of Solano County history. Writing a history column seemed like a good way to make use of all that material.

There is not any particular order or structure, subject matter or other format, other than a broad recounting of stories of people and events that circulated for years. Some of the stories are about matters of great significance while others fall under the heading of unusual and off-beat. You will not need a bookmark—just open this book randomly to find tales of tragedy, treachery, and crime, along with stories of heroism, bravery, and achievement. Throughout, I looked for more details and new research that would help to expand upon and improve some of the old accounts written by earlier Vallejo-area columnists and historians. I hope that putting these columns into book form will help to preserve some of our very colorful history and perhaps encourage future storytellers to do more research and unearth more details that will advance and improve what is written here.

1

2017 Columns

City of Vallejo's Colorful History Starts with Gen. Mariano Vallejo (May 13, 2017)

This is the first of many columns I hope to write about the Vallejo area's colorful and fascinating history. The idea is to focus on individuals who played important roles in our community, as well as sensational events that produced front-page news stories. Off-beat accounts about local characters and their deeds—whether good, brilliant, bad or just plain dumb—also are planned. Some columns might make you smile, others won't. It all comes under the heading of area history that ought to be remembered rather than forgotten. If you have a tale that fits in this category, pass it along. You can email me at genoans@hotmail.com or mail any material to me care of the *Times-Herald*, 420 Virginia St., Vallejo CA 94590, and make sure you include your phone number. Also, you can drop off any submissions at the Vallejo Naval and Historical Museum, around the corner from the *Times-Herald* at 734 Marin St.—the former City Hall for all you old-timers. The museum's extensive files will provide invaluable source material for these columns.

In writing about Vallejo history, a likely place to start is with Gen. Mariano Guadalupe Vallejo, a well-educated and far-thinking Californio who on Nov. 29, 1836, at age 29, became commandant general of Mexico's northern frontier. The title of "general" stuck, although Vallejo's highest military rank was that of colonel in the Mexican Army.

Vallejo had passed through our area a few years earlier, as a lieutenant with orders to find a site for a military post north of San Francisco Bay. For his efforts in helping to establish that post in Sonoma, creating a buffer between the Californians and Russians based at Fort Ross, he received a 66,000-acre land grant known as the Rancho Petaluma. Vallejo later received the 84,000-acre Rancho Suscol grant that encompassed the future sites of the city of Vallejo and Mare Island Naval Shipyard. Those ranchos plus additional grants eventually totaled more 170,000 acres—about 266 square miles—that extended from the Carquinez Strait to Mendocino County.

Mare Island was first named Isla Plana or Flat Island by Spanish explorers in 1775. Its current name, according to one generally accepted story, stems from a mishap in the Carquinez Strait involving a white mare belonging to Gen. Vallejo. One version has the mare falling off a crude raft and ending up on the island, and another version has the

Gen. Mariano Guadalupe Vallejo was a well-educated and far-thinking Californio who served as commandant general of Mexico's northern frontier. (*Vallejo Naval and Historical Museum*)

mare drifting away from horses that Vallejo's workers or soldiers were swimming across the strait. After the discovery of the horse on Isla Plana, Vallejo renamed the island Isla de la Yegua, or Island of the Mare.

Vallejo started the process that resulted in the city bearing his name while serving as a senator in the state of California's first legislative session. The lawmakers met on Dec. 15, 1849, in San Jose, prior to the formal Sept. 9, 1850, entry of the state into the Union. During that session he pushed for a permanent capital city at the south end of his Rancho Suscol. Vallejo, at that point considered the richest man in the state, offered 156 acres of land and $370,000 in gold to pay for construction of several government buildings.

Vallejo wanted the seat of state government named Eureka, but his friends in the Legislature decided to name the new city after him. Ultimately, the effort to make Vallejo the capital city of California failed. More will be written about that in a later column.

A disillusioned Gen. Vallejo sold the Vallejo townsite for $25,000 in 1854 to his son-in-law, John B. Frisbie, who was married to Vallejo's oldest daughter, Epifania. The dream of Vallejo as California's capital city was gone, but Frisbie worked hard to get the U.S. government to buy Mare Island for a West Coast naval base. The island was purchased in 1853 and the Navy base opened in 1854, with David Glasgow Farragut in charge as shipyard commandant.

Frisbie also tried to defend the title to Gen. Vallejo's Rancho Suscol land grant, which included the Vallejo townsite, but on March 24, 1862, the U.S. Supreme Court overturned a lower court's confirmation of the grant. Vallejo was reduced to his 228-acre Lachryma Montis homestead in Sonoma. He almost lost that to a lawyer who held a mortgage on the property, but Frisbie bought out the attorney and deeded the property to Vallejo's wife, Francisca Benicia Vallejo.

From the mid-1860s on, Vallejo made ends meet by renting out small plots of land for truck gardening and operated a water company that utilized a spring on his estate. He even mended fences and hauled wood. Vallejo remained a prominent figure, attending many public events as an honored guest or speaker. He served for several years on the state Board of Horticulture, wrote a five-volume *History of California*, commissioned paintings depicting that history, and collected many documents from native Californians that formed one of the cornerstones of the Bancroft Library. He died at his Lachryma Montis home on Jan. 18, 1890, at age 82.

Any good book on California history will mention Gen. Vallejo. The most current biography is General Vallejo and the Advent of the Americans, written by historian and university professor Alan Rosenus. Also, there's a wealth of information on Gen. Vallejo at the Vallejo Naval and Historical Museum.

John Frisbie, Gen. Vallejo's Son-in-law, Promoted City of Vallejo (May 27, 2017)

Gen. Mariano Vallejo, at one point a millionaire who owned vast tracts of Northern California land, ended up in tight financial circumstances after California entered the Union. His enterprising son-in-law, John Blackman Frisbie, helped to keep him in the comfort of his home in Sonoma—but also managed to nearly drive him to the poorhouse.

John Frisbie, considered the founder of the city of Vallejo, was both a help and a hindrance to his father-in-law, Gen. Mariano Vallejo. (*Vallejo Naval and Historical Museum*)

Frisbie, an Army captain, arrived in Sonoma in mid-1848, in charge of a rough-and-tumble company of New York volunteers. Educated in law and ambitious, Frisbie mustered out of the Army following the end to the Mexican-American War. He stayed in the Sonoma area, quickly learned Spanish and was drawn into Vallejo's family circle and business affairs. In 1850 Frisbie obtained Vallejo's power of attorney, which gave him a significant amount of control over the general's finances, and in 1851 married the general's oldest daughter, Epifania or Fannie.

Frisbie is widely considered the founder of the city of Vallejo, given his significant role in planning and promoting the new city that bears his father-in-law's name. With Frisbie's help, Gen. Vallejo found investors who said they would underwrite his efforts to make Vallejo the capital city of California. Two legislative sessions began in the new city, in early 1852 and 1853, only to reconvene in Benicia and Sacramento because of inadequate preparations in Vallejo. Gen. Vallejo had spent nearly $100,000 of his own funds on the capital city project, but the other investors didn't deliver on their promises. Disillusioned, he sold Frisbie the Vallejo townsite for $25,000 in 1854.

While the dream of a capital city was gone, Frisbie had been working hard to get the U.S. government to buy Mare Island for a West Coast naval base. The island was purchased in 1853 and the Navy base opened in 1854. At the start of the Civil War, one of the new Union military units was the Vallejo Rifles, mustered in on Sept. 8, 1861. Frisbie was appointed the first captain of the unit. He was promoted to the rank of general by Gov. Leland Stanford in 1862, and the title remained with him for the rest of his life.

Frisbie didn't have a formal law practice in California but did get involved in some important legal cases, including the effort to defend the title to Gen. Vallejo's 84,000-acre Rancho Suscol land grant, which included the Vallejo townsite. On March 24, 1862, the U.S. Supreme Court overturned a lower court's confirmation of the grant. Using his lobbying skills, Frisbie pushed successfully for a bill, approved by Congress in 1863, that enabled him and some friends to retain their Suscol land grant holdings by buying land at the government price of $1.25 an acre. That worked for men with ready cash, but not for Gen. Vallejo who already was paying high interest on mortgages—mortgages that Frisbie had expedited.

Gen. Vallejo and his wife, Dona Francisca Benicia, were at times bitter about what they considered Frisbie's mismanagement. Dona Francisca, in a letter to her son Platon, called Frisbie an "ingrate" and added, "but he is an American and we can't hope for anything but tricks."

But Frisbie came through for the Vallejos in 1866, when Vallejo lost his 228-acre Lachryma Montis homestead in Sonoma. Thomas Madden, one of the lawyers who had represented him during the hearings on his Suscol land grant case, held a $17,500 mortgage on the estate and assumed ownership when Vallejo couldn't pay off the note. The general had to rent the property for $150 a month. But in late 1871, Frisbie paid Madden $21,000 for Lachryma Montis and four months later deeded the property to Francisca Benicia Vallejo.

In overseeing the development of the city of Vallejo, Frisbie had control of local transportation, banking and farming interests. He also donated land for the construction of the community's first public school, city park and cemetery; and donated land to many of Vallejo's early churches. But in 1876, Frisbie went broke. His banking institution, the Vallejo Savings and Commercial Bank, had invested heavily in Bonanza stocks. When those stocks spiraled downward, he began selling off assets to satisfy creditors. Those assets included the Bernard Hotel in Vallejo and the White Sulphur Springs resort, now known as Blue Rock Springs, east of the town. He also lost his own private estate, a mansion on the southeast corner of Virginia and Sutter streets, overlooking the town of Vallejo.

In 1878, Frisbie left with his wife and children for Mexico, where he befriended and worked for President Porfirio Diaz—and became richer than he had been in California. One of his biggest achievements for Diaz was a lobbying effort that led to the reversal of a hostile U.S. trade policy toward Mexico. The president rewarded him with a generous fee and an old gold mine that hadn't been worked for 200 or more years. Frisbie and a partner developed the property and it made them millionaires. Frisbie remained a prominent figure in Mexico for many years. He died in Mexico City in May 1909, at age 85.

While Frisbie is buried in Mexico City, the tallest monument in Vallejo's old St. Vincent's Cemetery bears his name. The lone grave marker in the family plot bears the name of Frisbie's son, Mariano Guadalupe Frisbie, who died at age four in the Napa Valley in 1856. More information on John Frisbie is available at the Vallejo Naval and Historical Museum, 734 Marin St. Also, there is a great deal of information on Frisbie in General Vallejo and the Advent of the Americans, authored by Alan Rosenus.

Admiral David Farragut, First Mare Island Shipyard Commandant (June 10, 2017)

Mare Island's long tenure as the U.S. Navy's first base on the West Coast began in 1850, two months after California's Sept. 9, 1850, entry into the Union, when the island was reserved for military use by President Millard Fillmore. A survey in 1852 resulted in a recommendation that the island be turned into a naval base, and the island was purchased for $83,491 on Jan. 4, 1853.

Commander David Glasgow Farragut, with orders to serve as the first commandant of Mare Island Naval Shipyard, arrived on Sept. 16, 1854, ran off several squatters and took charge. With the Navy's arrival, Vallejo's future course was set.

The choice of Farragut to create the shipyard turned out to be a wise move. Farragut, commandant from 1854 to 1858, transformed a desolate site into a bustling Navy base capable of handling the many types of ship repair work done by long-established East Coast Navy yards.

Farragut was just 9½ years old when he was appointed a Navy midshipman in 1810. By the time he arrived at Mare Island, he had more than 40 years of service at sea and at the Navy's Norfolk shipyard behind him. He was stationed on the USS *Essex* during the War of 1812 and served as master of a captured British ship, the HMS *Barclay*, when he was only 12. Farragut and other Essex crew members were captured and held prisoner for several months in 1814 after a bloody battle against British warships that killed 58 Essex sailors.

After the war, Farragut served in U.S. fleets in the Mediterranean and the Caribbean, had command of a ship in the Gulf of Mexico during the Mexican-American War, and had three tours of duty at the Norfolk Navy Yard. He spent four years as Mare Island commandant and then returned to sea duty. By the eve of the Civil War, he was nearing retirement from a successful, though not celebrated, Navy career. But he wanted new

David Glasgow Farragut was the first commandant of Mare Island Naval Shipyard. He went on to become a Civil War hero and the navy's first admiral. (*Vallejo Naval and Historical Museum*)

orders, was given command of a newly commissioned sloop-of-war, the USS *Hartford*, and became a Civil War hero. He had a key role in capturing the port of New Orleans in April 1862, failed to capture Vicksburg on the Mississippi later that year, and then achieved fame with a critical Union victory at the Battle of Mobile Bay in August 1864—where he's remembered for saying, "Damn the torpedoes, full speed ahead!"

That's close to what he actually said, which was, "Damn the torpedoes! Four bells! Capt. Drayton, go ahead! Jouett, full speed!"

Farragut's decision to order his fleet into perilous Mobile Bay waters filled with torpedoes—actually submerged mines—was risky. One of his four ironclad monitors, the USS *Tecumseh*, struck a mine and went down. Had his wooden ship been hit and sunk, he and many of the ship's crew could have drowned. Resulting confusion could have led to a Union loss instead of an important victory. Instead of emerging from the battle a courageous hero, he could have been labeled reckless and foolhardy. But good fortune was on his side.

Farragut's fleet, minus the *Tecumseh*, made it into Mobile Bay and, after some resistance, forced the Confederate ships in the bay to surrender or flee. Over the next three weeks, shelling by Farragut's ships and gun and artillery fire by Union Army soldiers finally forced the Confederate defenders of Fort Morgan, at the entrance to Mobile Bay, to surrender. Though the city of Mobile remained in Confederate hands into 1865, Farragut had achieved a major goal: the port was closed to rebel blockade runners.

After the victory, Farragut was promoted to vice-admiral and grateful citizens of New York raised a $50,000 gift of bonds for him—the equivalent of nearly $1 million today. In 1866, Congress promoted Farragut a final time by creating the new rank of admiral. After the war, Farragut and his wife Virginia went on a triumphant world tour and in August 1869 made an official visit to Mare Island. He also had a hero's welcome in Vallejo, which in 15 years had grown from a tiny village to a town of more than 6,000 residents, and visited Gen. Mariano Vallejo in Sonoma. A year later, on Aug. 14, 1870, Farragut died at age 69 in Portsmouth, N.H.

Farragut has been commemorated with a statue in Washington, D.C., five Navy ships named for him over the years, and other honors. But, as stated in *A Long Line of Ships*, Arnold Lott's book about Mare Island, it's on the old shipyard and in Vallejo where he may be best remembered. Lott's book and other material on Farragut can be found at the Vallejo Naval and Historical Museum, at 734 Marin Street, and at the Mare Island Museum, 1100 Railroad Ave., on Mare Island.

Vallejo Served as California's Capital City—But Not for Long (June 25, 2017)

Gen. Mariano Vallejo had big dreams for the city that bears his name. He started the process that led to brief capital city status for Vallejo while serving as a senator in the state of California's first legislative session. The lawmakers met on Dec. 15, 1849, in San Jose, prior to the formal Sept. 9, 1850, entry of the state into the Union. During that session he pushed for a permanent capital city at the south end of his 84,000-acre Rancho Suscol land grant. Vallejo, at that point considered the richest man in the state, offered 156 acres of land along the Napa River and $370,000 in gold to pay for construction of several government buildings. His plans called for a Capitol building, state offices, state library, university, schools, hospitals, orphanages and gardens. There were few doubts about his ability to fulfill his promises.

Vallejo wanted the seat of state government named Eureka, but his friends in the Legislature decided to name the new city after him. On Oct. 7, 1850, California voters overwhelmingly supported the location, casting 7,477 votes for the Vallejo location. San Jose ran a distant second with 1,292 votes.

California's second legislative session convened in January 1851, still in San Jose as Vallejo tried to complete his ambitious building project. But there were signs of trouble as the lawmakers adjourned on May 1 and started planning for their third session, scheduled to open on Jan. 5, 1852, in Vallejo. Gov. John McDougall had ordered the state offices and archives moved to Vallejo without prior legislative approval or an adequate review of the construction, and by September 1851 realized that work on the Capitol building was moving slowly. He proposed a return to San Jose, but lawmakers, meeting in San Francisco a week before the formal start of the third session, voted 28-13 for Vallejo.

When the third session opened on Jan. 5 in Vallejo, the legislators encountered an unfinished wood-frame building atop York Street Hill, with seating improvised from nail kegs or benches made by laying boards on stools. Three days later enough chairs arrived. Inadequate hotel accommodations were described by an Alta California

The capitol of California, depicted in an 1857 painting by Felix Mathews, stood atop Vallejo's York Street Hill overlooking Mare Island Strait. The wood-frame structure was destroyed by fire in 1859. (*Vallejo Naval and Historical Museum*)

newspaper correspondent as "villainous." The writer quipped that three legislators, with no place to sleep, sat in chairs until nearly frozen, then ran around to warm up and repeated the process until morning. The steamer *Empire*, which brought many of the lawmakers to Vallejo, became a floating boarding house for people who had to trudge through mud to reach the statehouse. Legislators had been in session for only one week when they voted on Jan. 12 to leave town. On Jan. 16, the *Empire* cast off, packed with legislators and others, bound for Sacramento for the rest of the session.

The 1852 move to Sacramento was temporary, not permanent, and legislators returned to Vallejo on Jan. 3, 1853, for the start of California's fourth session. But dissatisfaction with conditions multiplied and the lawmakers voted on Feb. 4 to move to Benicia. But Benicia couldn't hang onto its new status either. After the fifth legislative session convened there on Jan. 2, 1854, there were more complaints about lack of improvements, scarce accommodations and high prices. One reason for poor accommodations was that Sacramento advocates came up with a scheme to tie up available rooms: sending a couple hundred men to Benicia to rent many of the available hotel and boarding house rooms just before the lawmakers arrived. Sacramento advocates then succeeded in pushing through a bill to make their city the capital of California. On Feb. 25, legislators in Benicia voted to adjourn and meet on March 1 in Sacramento. Except for flooding in Sacramento in 1862 that forced lawmakers to shift for a few months to San Francisco, the days of a drifting California capital were over.

The statehouse building atop York Street Hill in Vallejo was used for several years by local farmers for hay storage, and the basement was divided into small apartments. A fire started in one of the apartments in June 1859, spread to the hay and the entire building was destroyed in a matter of minutes. York Street Hill is gone—bulldozed flat in the 1960s during the city's massive redevelopment project. The approximate location of the statehouse is marked by a plaque at the downtown Transit Center, 311 Sacramento St., and a couple of pavement stamps at the nearby corner of Sacramento and York streets.

If you're looking for more information on California's migrating capital cities, read *The Capital That Couldn't Stay Put* by June Oxford. It's packed with details about the state's wandering early-day legislators. Information on Vallejo's capital-city status also can be found at the Vallejo Naval and Historical Museum, at 734 Marin St.

Early-day Vallejo Judge Browne Liked to Tell Tall Tales (July 16, 2017)

Research into Vallejo history can get complicated—especially when you encounter someone whose writings about the city's earliest days were based, as they say these days, on alternative facts. That's what you find in reading Vallejo Police Judge John Browne's *Early Days* memoir.

Browne's version of Vallejo history is a mixture of what is generally known to be true—along with details "that are neither mentioned or verified elsewhere," as a 1989 *Solano Historian* article states. That's a polite way of saying that Browne, known as "Judge Ha Ha" because of his humorous asides, at times was full of baloney.

Browne, born in Vallejo in 1859, wrote accurately about the first streets and buildings in Vallejo, down to the location of his home at 208 York Street. But you have to wonder about his tale of Swedes Ole and Katrina Johnson being the first non-Indian, non-Hispanic residents of what later became Vallejo.

Johnson was a sailor on a ship that in the mid-1840s docked at Acapulco, where he met and married Katrina, the daughter of the Swedish consul, Browne wrote. After sailing to San Francisco, they jumped ship and made their way up the bay in a leaky boat to Vallejo, which they named Eden. Gen. Mariano Vallejo instead wanted to call the place Eureka, but California lawmakers finally decided to name the place after him.

Well, only Browne came up with the story of the Johnsons' arrival—a story that some historians later accepted. However, as the *Solano Historian* notes, Ole's name isn't included in Browne's own list of area pioneers, or in historian H.H. Bancroft's list of California residents prior to 1848. And, by the way, no Swedish consulate existed in Acapulco when Ole supposedly sailed into port there.

Browne also had a funny version of how California's Great Seal was adopted by the state Legislature. "Judge Ha Ha" claimed that Gen. Vallejo suggested the seal depict a beautiful, naked blonde —looking a lot like the alleged Katrina Johnson—sitting on a rock, with three Indians offering her an apple and Ole digging clams in the background. Browne said the senators were too narrow-minded to accept Vallejo's suggestions, except to include the word Eureka. Yes, the approved seal depicts a woman, but she's a clothed Roman goddess Minerva (Athena in Greek mythology) holding a spear and a shield.

His sense of humor also was evident in an Oct. 31, 1921, *Vallejo Evening Chronicle* story that said Browne, during his tenure as a police judge, wanted to arrange a contract between the city and the Vallejo Yacht Club to buy contraband booze seized in Prohibition-era police raids and use the liquor to remove barnacles and old paint from boats.

Early-day Vallejo Police Judge John Browne, standing, keeps an eye on the poker game at the Vallejo Yacht Club in the early 1900s. The gamblers were author Jack London (right) and George Hilton. (*Vallejo Naval and Historical Museum*)

"After endangering his olfactory organs this morning while determining that certain evidence in bottles was indeed 'likker,' Judge Browne declared that the stuff would quickly remove barnacles and paint from copper bottoms of boats but would have to be removed quickly if the owners of the boats want to save the hulls," the newspaper article stated.

There's no baloney regarding Browne's longstanding friendship with famed author Jack London, a Vallejo Yacht Club member. A photo hanging on the wall at the club shows London playing cards there, with Browne standing next to him. Friendly letters the two sent to one another have turned up in recent years in Jack London memorabilia auctions. Browne's 30-foot sloop was named the Charmian, after London's wife.

Browne also got into a war of words with Capt. Harry George, a Mare Island shipyard commandant who was strongly opposed to the various forms of gambling that Navy sailors encountered while on liberty in Vallejo.

In a Nov. 1, 1918, court decision, Browne imposed a small $10 fine on a man who was running a Chinese lottery in Vallejo's Lower Georgia Street district. Browne also accused Navy investigators who developed the case of trying to "purify" Vallejo while shipyard officials were running their own gambling games in the form of raffles to promote sales of "Liberty Loan" bonds.

An irate Capt. George followed up with a lengthy letter denying that he was trying to purify Vallejo. He said Navy investigators had turned up enough evidence to justify arrests of 25 people, most in the Lower Georgia district, for violations of various laws. Capt. George also said Browne's courtroom action displayed "a temperamental unfitness to perform judicial duties."

In a rambling response, Browne said he checked with the federal Treasury Department regarding Mare Island shipyard raffles to promote Liberty Bond sales and was advised that the agency didn't countenance such activity. The judge said that the "Purity Squad" on Mare Island wasn't doing anything about the shipyard workers playing "the seductive game of 'Craps,' the stakes running from a collar button to a Liberty Bond." He also told Capt. George that as "an abettor of gambling you appear raw and astringent as the ordinary craps shooter."

It didn't end there. Browne said he wanted to avoid "any personal reflection"—and then said that years earlier Capt. George, as a young Navy ensign, was known in the Lower Georgia district as a "'rough-neck" because of his "nightly or frequent orgies of disreputable associations and reprehensible actions … you were a strange compound of officer probity and public grossness."

In Marguerite Hune's *History of Solano County, California*, Browne is described as one of the county's best-known and most popular residents. Hune says Browne "married happily more couples than all of the judges combined in Solano County," and also was a judge in many "beautiful baby" contests.

Besides his public service as a police judge, justice of the peace and city trustee, Browne helped to organize and run the yacht club, operated a candy company, was active in the Native Sons of the Golden West, had a private law practice and worked as a notary public until a few weeks before his death in 1937 at age 78. He was, as Lee Fountain wrote in the *Solano Historian*, "a conspicuous figure in Vallejo's early history." Hune's book and Fountain's article, along with other information on Browne, can be found at the Vallejo Naval and Historical Museum.

Civil War Plots Involved Vallejo, Benicia, Napa, San Francisco (Sept. 3, 2017)

Some historians say the danger of California declaring for the Confederacy during the Civil War was exaggerated and that political sentiment was overwhelmingly pro-Union. But newspapers in the 1860s had many reports of rumored and actual rebel plots in the state—including schemes in the San Francisco, Vallejo, Benicia and Napa areas.

Control of Mare Island Naval Shipyard, across the Napa River from Vallejo, was a key factor during the Civil War. Ships could be repaired and supplied, and the shipyard had a floating drydock capable of handling ocean-going vessels. Because of concerns that Mare Island might be seized by Confederate sympathizers, about 100 Marines were ordered to report to the shipyard. They left New York aboard the mail steamer Ariel in late 1862, only to be captured six days later near Cuba by the CSS *Alabama*. The Marines were released on the condition they not fight against Confederate soldiers, and the Ariel continued on its way after posting of a $261,000 ransom bond.

The Marines finally reached Mare Island on Jan. 1, 1863—none too soon. One month later, a group of Southern sympathizers in San Francisco purchased the *J.M. Chapman*, a fast schooner, for $6,500 and began fitting it out as a privateer to prey on ships hauling fortunes in gold to the East Coast. There was very little Navy protection for these "treasure ships," and the plan was to use the gold to help finance the Confederacy. One of the conspirators, Asbury Harpending, had met the previous year with Confederacy President Jefferson Davis in Richmond, Va., to outline the daring plot. Harpending, who

Early-day photo of Marines in front of the marine officers' quarters on Mare Island Naval Shipyard. Marines were sent to Mare Island during the Civil War because of fears that Southern sympathizers might try to seize the shipyard. (*Mare Island Museum*)

had made a fortune in California's gold fields, also proposed seizing the Army's Benicia Arsenal and Mare Island. He wanted to use three Navy ships based at Mare Island to attack San Francisco. Harpending faced long odds, but he believed that if everything fell into place the South could claim California.

On March 15, the *J.M. Chapman*, secretly loaded with cases of 12-pound cannonballs, howitzer shells, rifles, pistols, cutlasses and other weapons, headed from its San Francisco dock toward the Golden Gate. But the skipper hired for the ship had been too talkative while drinking in a bar on shore, and authorities were ready. Two boats full of Marines pursued and boarded the schooner as the USS *Cyane*, a sloop-of-war that had recently arrived for repairs at Mare Island, trained its guns on the conspirators. In addition to a *J.M. Chapman* deck crew of several men, 15 more armed men were found hiding below decks. They surrendered without firing a shot. Instead of the open sea and easy targets, the plotters wound up in cells on Alcatraz.

Two days later, the sheriff of Napa County came to Mare Island with the disturbing news that Southern sympathizers in his area had been plotting an attack on Mare Island. The Alta California newspaper reported on March 28 that 200 or more secessionists had banded together for the attack on the shipyard and also on the Benicia Arsenal. High security was established at both locations, but the rebels from Napa never showed up.

In late April, the *Philadelphia Inquirer* editorialized that the Napa County plot at first seemed like "an insane enterprise of a few of the rascals who still infest that new county. It seems, however, that there was 'method in their madness.'" Had all the plots, including the Chapman privateering, succeeded, "even a momentary success would have been a heavy blow to the Union cause, and a serious damage to the Pacific coast," the *Inquirer* added.

In the city of Napa, the secessionist threat had been considered strong enough to warrant formation of artillery, infantry and cavalry companies. "This small army almost went to war once, when it was informed that men were conducting artillery drills with a fieldpiece near Yountville," Arnold Lott wrote in *A Long Line of Ships*, his book about Mare Island. "Scouts were dispatched to spy out the enemy—who proved to be only a few fellows having themselves some fun with a piece of stovepipe and a pair of wagon wheels."

"How many Southern sympathizers there were in the valleys north of Vallejo, or what their actual plans were, no one ever learned," Lott said. "With victory won by the North, there was but little satisfaction to be gained in hashing over the details of a lost cause."

In Benicia, there had been concerns about secessionist activity dating to the start of the war in 1861. In January of that year, Col. Albert Sidney Johnston was appointed as commander of the U.S. Department of the Pacific, in charge of the Benicia Arsenal as well as Fort Point and Alcatraz in San Francisco Bay. Despite Johnston's great military experience, his Southern roots and association with Jefferson Davis prior to the war undermined the public's faith in his commitment to the Union cause. There were rumors that local confederates had actually met with him to discuss plans to raid the Benicia Arsenal for weapons and attack Mare Island and San Francisco. Johnston swore to his Union allegiance, and took actions at Benicia and San Francisco that proved it, but less than two weeks after the April 12, 1861, start of the Civil War the Army relieved him of his post. Johnston rode home on horseback to the South with a contingent of volunteers, and accepted a commission as a general in the Confederate Army. A year later, he died at the battle of Shiloh as one of the heroes of the Confederacy.

Gangster George "Baby Face" Nelson Hung Out in Vallejo in the 1930s (Sept. 17, 2017)

A federal court trial in San Francisco in 1935 brought to light the little-known fact that George "Baby Face" Nelson, at one point the FBI's Public Enemy No. 1, was one of several infamous gangsters and their associates who were in and out of Vallejo during the 1930s.

The gangsters' connection was Thomas "Tobe" Williams, who ran the town's only hospital, Vallejo General Hospital, on Tennessee Street. The hospital's reputation as a stopping place for notorious criminals wasn't widely known until the details emerged in the federal court proceedings against Williams and others for harboring Nelson while he was on the run.

"Tobe" Williams, born Tobias Cohen in 1862, served prison time for a Montana burglary. His right leg had been amputated above the knee, and one story was that he lost the leg in a bungled attempt to blast open a bank safe. In 1914, Williams purchased Vallejo's first hospital, at the corner of Virginia Street and Sonoma Boulevard. In 1922, with community support and a local bank loan, he opened a new, larger hospital on Tennessee Street that served the community for decades.

The 6-foot 7-inch Williams was much more than a hospital owner and manager. Besides serving residents of Vallejo, his hospital took care of sick or wounded fugitives who didn't have to worry about being bothered by local authorities. Williams, according to FBI reports, said he had good political connections in Vallejo and would be quickly alerted if any federal authorities were coming to town.

George "Baby Face" Nelson and other infamous gangsters hung out in Vallejo during the 1930s. During part of the time that he was in and out of Vallejo, Nelson was the FBI's Public Enemy No. 1. (*Vallejo Naval and Historical Museum*)

Some Vallejo residents knew or had heard rumors about Williams' background and associations. Dr. Edward A. Peterson, in an FBI interview, recalled a conversation with hospital nurse Lorena Slater, who said, "It is the most terrible thing I have ever heard that the boss should allow people like that ('Baby Face' Nelson) to come in here." Peterson also said the nurse referred to Alvin "Creepy" Karpis, a Barker-Karpis gang leader who had his tonsils removed at Vallejo General in February 1933, as one of the "bums" that Williams allowed into the hospital.

According to the FBI, Nelson regularly stopped to visit Williams while traveling between California and Nevada, trying to evade authorities or transporting liquor to Reno during the Prohibition era. Besides Karpis, the FBI's fourth and last Public Enemy No. 1 after Nelson's death, Nelson's wife Helen twice was a patient at the hospital. A federal agent walked into the hospital on Oct. 11, 1934, and saw Barker gang member Chuck Fitzgerald, who was recovering from a gunshot wound, but failed to recognize him at the time. In late 1933, Arthur "Doc" Barker was treated for a wound that caused one of his fingers to get infected. Other patients included Reno underworld figures Bill "Curly" Graham, Jim "Shorty" McKay, and Henry "Tex" Hall. Kate "Ma" Barker also visited Williams in Vallejo, according to the FBI. Others who stopped from time to time to see Williams included bootlegger Joe "Soap" Moreno and Joseph "Fatso" Negri, who had been a trusted member of Nelson's gang.

When Nelson's wife was hospitalized, he stayed in the Casa de Vallejo, the town's best hotel. Negri told FBI agents that he and the Nelsons also stayed at the Dodgin Auto Court, on Broadway Street just off Tennessee Street, in late September and early October, 1934, and while there they walked downtown to see a movie before driving to Reno. On their way to Reno, the Nelsons and Negri realized they accidentally took a blanket from the auto court and stopped to call the auto court owners to tell them, "we were mailing it back to them parcel post from Sacramento."

Williams and three co-defendants were convicted April 5, 1935, of harboring Nelson. Federal Judge Walter Lindley imposed the harshest sentence on Williams: a $5,000 fine and an 18-month prison term. He was sentenced to prison despite offering a petition, signed by 119 Vallejo residents, asking for clemency on the ground that he was not guilty of harboring "of his own free will and accord." Williams was released after serving a year in McNeil Island federal prison in Washington state.

After his release from prison, Williams returned to his post as general manager of his hospital. When Williams died on July 7, 1942, at age 80 after a protracted illness, newspaper obituaries made only brief mention of his past gangland connections.

Nelson, born Lester Joseph Gillis, became Public Enemy No. 1 following the death of one of his crime partners, John Dillinger, in a July 22, 1934, FBI ambush. After leaving Vallejo in early October that year, Nelson went to Nevada and then headed for the Midwest. He died following a Nov. 27, 1934, shootout with the FBI in Barrington, Ill. The 5-foot-4 gangster, whose murder victims included three FBI agents, was described by author Bryan Burrough, in his book *Public Enemies: America's Greatest Crime Wave and the Birth of the FBI, 1933–34*, as "the most violent of the Depression-era outlaws, a manic multiple murderer who drew disdain even as Dillinger and Pretty Boy Floyd attained the status of folk heroes."

More details of Nelson's activity in Vallejo and his dealings with "Tobe" Williams are included in my book, *Lower Georgia Street: California's Forgotten Barbary Coast*.

Chief or Not, Solano Was Important Ally of Gen. Vallejo (Oct. 15, 2017)

In writing about "Chief" Solano, Solano County's namesake and Gen. Mariano Vallejo's ally and loyal friend, separating fact from fiction can be difficult—mainly because of exaggerations and misstatements by Vallejo that for many decades were accepted as gospel.

One of the grandiose comments from Vallejo was in a report to California legislators in 1850 describing Solano as "the great Chief of the tribes originally denominated Suisunes." Not so, say several historians and researchers who have looked beyond Gen. Vallejo's statements.

It's true that Solano, who at 6-foot-7 dwarfed the 5-foot-4 Vallejo, helped Vallejo quell tribal uprisings in the 1830s. Vallejo, as commandant general of Mexico's northern frontier, definitely needed that help in protecting Californio settlers. But to call Solano a great Suisun chief doesn't match up with the record developed in recent years by Dr. Randall Milliken, M. Clyde Low, Jerry Bowen and James Ramirez, among others.

Their research shows that Solano first appears in Spanish records not as a warrior but as a 10- or 11-year-old boy named Sina, who was one of the survivors of a May 1810 attack on the Suisun tribe, near present-day Rockville, by soldiers led by Lt. Gabriel Moraga. Sina was taken to Mission Dolores in San Francisco, where he was baptized the following July as Francisco Solano. Moraga was ordered to attack the Suisuns because they were believed to have killed 16 members of nearby tribes who had converted to Christianity.

Sculptor William Huff and his statue of "Chief" Solano, about 1934. With no photos of Solano, Huff said his interpretation was "a figment of my own imagination." (*Vallejo Naval and Historical Museum*)

24

Vallejo also said Sina was known as Sem-Yeto, signifying "brave of fierce hand," prior to his baptism. But the "tough guy" characterization doesn't suit a boy—even a tall one like Sina.

In 1824, Solano was sent to the Mission San Francisco Solano at Sonoma and soon became an *alcalde*, one of several missionary-controlled headmen of that mission. By the mid-1830s, he was still an *alcalde*, and head of an 18-member family household.

Other tales include Vallejo's description of a dangerous confrontation he had with Solano, who was leading several thousand American Indians. Vallejo had only about 200 Mexican soldiers. But instead of a battle there was a negotiation and truce. None of that ever happened, Bowen says. Even early-day California historian H. H. Bancroft said the stand-off, as reported by Vallejo, was "greatly exaggerated if not purely imaginary."

Another story now dismissed as fable tells of Solano's alleged attempt to kidnap a Russian princess from Fort Ross. But Vallejo saves the day, showing up to stop Solano. Ramirez says that tale came from Gen. Vallejo's son, Dr. Platon Vallejo, who had a "penchant for testing the limits of credulity."

Other accounts depict Solano, horseback and in a full-dress Mexican Army uniform, with an honor guard of other uniformed American Indians, giving rousing speeches to fire up his troops before heading off to a battle. That's possible, Bowen says, noting that Vallejo had commissioned Solano as an Army captain.

Bancroft also wrote that Vallejo arranged for Solano and about 80 other uniformed warriors to travel with him in 1836 to Monterey to impress and seek military support from Juan Bautista Alvarado, Mexican governor of Alta California. Vallejo went to Monterey, but Bancroft said he didn't know whether Solano and his troops actually made the ride.

In 1837, for helping Vallejo deal with tribal uprisings, Solano received a provisional Mexican land grant of about 17,000 acres that included his homeland in the Rockville area. The land grant coincided with plagues of smallpox and cholera that decimated the Suisuns, leaving only a few hundred survivors. The official title to Rancho Suisun was granted to Solano in January 1842, and a few months later Vallejo bought the land for the equivalent of $1,000. "It appears that crafty old Gen. Vallejo's intention all along was to acquire the Suisun Rancho for his own use," Bowen writes. In 1850, Vallejo sold the land to Archibald Ritchie for $50,000.

When the Bear Flag Revolt resulted in Vallejo being imprisoned at Sutter's Fort in mid-1846, Solano dropped out of sight, apparently fearing that his old friend had died. He returned in 1850, reunited with Vallejo, and then returned to the Rockville area where he became ill and died. Various reports over the years placed his burial site under a buckeye tree along what's now Suisun Valley Road, near Rockville. Bowen says human bones found in that area were reburied at a nearby Solano Community College location. That site is marked by a bronze plaque.

Solano is commemorated by a bust outside the John F. Kennedy Library in Vallejo, and by a 12-foot-tall bronze statue, now in front of the Solano County Events Center in Fairfield. Neither one is considered an accurate portrayal of Solano. A bas-relief carving by Dr. Platon Vallejo, who as a boy knew Solano, is believed to be a better image. No confirmed photographs of Solano are known to exist.

A bronze tablet, which disappeared years ago, at the base of the Fairfield statue quoted Gen. Vallejo as saying, "To the bravery and in particular to the diplomacy of that great chieftain of the Suisun Indians, civilization is indeed indebted for the conquest of the territory which today comprises the counties of Solano, Napa, Sonoma and Lake." Bowen says those lofty words are partly accurate—Vallejo's taming of the four-county area ultimately would have succeeded, but it would have been a much more difficult and bloody process without the help he received from Solano and other tribal allies who were given weapons, uniforms and horses to help protect the Californios.

USS *California* Ran Aground on Mare Island Launch Day (Nov. 12, 2017)

Stories of the 624-foot USS *California*, the biggest ship ever built at Mare Island, almost cruising up Georgia Street in Vallejo on its launch day have been recounted time and again over the years. With the 98th anniversary of the Nov. 20, 1919, launch nearing, it's time to tell the tale again.

Some interesting details about the launching, not included in numerous earlier stories about Mare Island's only battleship, are in an official U.S. Navy report, dated Feb. 18, 1921, found in the files at the Vallejo Naval and Historical Museum.

The report has an exact launching timetable that states it took just under two minutes for the 32,600-ton battleship, classified as a super-dreadnought, to slide down the shipyard ways, cross the 1,230-foot-wide Mare Island Strait and run aground in Vallejo-side mud, ramming a ferry slip and forcing many frightened spectators to flee.

The launch ways appear to have a gentle incline into the narrow strait, but the USS *California* moved rapidly down that long ramp which had been heavily greased in advance. The report states that nearly 47,000 pounds of beef tallow and grease, plus 100 gallons of lard oil, were used.

USS *California* ran aground in Vallejo-side mud minutes after its November 20, 1919, launching at Mare Island Naval Shipyard. (*Dann Shively collection*)

26

For a few seconds, the ship was moving at about 25 feet per second, or nearly 17 miles per hour (just under 15 knots for the nautical types). And even as it slowed in the water, it was still moving too fast to avoid the Vallejo shoreline, lined with more than 1,000 people, and the Six Minute Ferry Co. ferry slip at the foot of Georgia Street. It took 10 tugboats 24 minutes to drag the undamaged California off the mud and get the ship started toward the Mare Island seawall.

Why didn't an elaborate braking and emergency anchor system work, and stop the ship about 350 feet away from the foot of Georgia Street as planned? The report states that defective welds caused links in each of 10 massive restraining chains to snap as the brakes were applied. Two back-up emergency anchors were dropped but not in time to stop the ship. The restraining chains were linked to metal cables that in turn ran through steel castings at the shipbuilding ways that could exert more than 1,100 pounds of braking pressure per square inch on the lines. It all looked good on paper and in pre-launch testing of a to-scale model of the ship.

"If we had the launching to do over again tomorrow, the only change that would be considered in the entire plan would be the use of wire cables to the brakes instead of the chains," Lt. Cmdr. Harold Saunders, in charge of the braking apparatus, said afterwards.

Saunders and Navy Capt. Henry Gleason had developed the intricate braking system, and had detailed it in a paper, "The Launching of Large Vessels in Restricted Waters," submitted to a national gathering of naval architects and engineers held in New York City only a week before the launching. Their guest at the launch was Capt. R. Stocker, the Navy's highest authority on ship construction. The *Vallejo Evening Chronicle*, in a pre-launch story, said the three officers would likely discuss ideas that "will result in changes being made for future building of dreadnought type of vessels." Mare Island Naval Shipyard wanted those changes to include more battleship construction at the shipyard, but the USS *California* problems did nothing to help achieve that goal.

In 1920, the keel for another battleship, the USS *Montana*, was laid at Mare Island— but about a year later work was halted. The partially completed Montana hull eventually was broken up. Many more ships were built at Mare Island after that, including the heavy cruisers Chicago and San Francisco—but no more battleships.

For years after the launching of the California, there were stories of the ship that "went half-way up Georgia Street," Arnold Lott wrote in *A Long Line of Ships*, his book about the history of Mare Island. "Spectators on the Vallejo side of the channel took one look at the mountain of steel moving relentlessly toward them, and suddenly remembered urgent business elsewhere."

It wasn't just the oncoming ship that prompted spectators to run. Bert Frazier, who witnessed the 1919 events, said in a *Vallejo Times-Herald* account years later that the battleship launching created a wave that rolled across the strait and broke "with unrestrained fury" on the Vallejo waterfront, sending water and spray 20 feet in the air.

Area historian Jerry Bowen wrote in a 2000 article that despite the California's "ignoble beginnings," briefly stuck in the mud on the Vallejo waterfront, it later earned its "rightful place in history as a magnificent battleship."

The flagship of the Navy's Pacific Fleet for 20 years, the *California* was torpedoed and sank on Dec. 7, 1941, during the Pearl Harbor attack, and 105 of her crew members died. The ship was salvaged and reconstructed, and went on to serve for the remainder of World War II.

The battleship was involved in the capture and occupation of Saipan, and saw action in the Philippines and the historic battle at Surigao Straits, where an entire arm of the Japanese Fleet was destroyed. The *California* was credited with sinking a Japanese battleship in that battle. Before it was all over, the ship was targeted by a Japanese kamikaze pilot who flew his plane into the aft control tower, killing 52 crewmen and injuring 153 others.

The *California* also participated in other historic sea battles at Guam, Tinian and Leyte Gulf. In 1946 she was retired to the Reserve Fleet at Philadelphia, and in 1959 was sold for $859,999, towed to Baltimore and scrapped.

Prohibition Shut Down Vallejo Saloons—But Booze Kept Flowing (Nov. 26, 2017)

A century ago, on Dec. 18, 1917, Congress passed the 18th Amendment, prohibiting the "manufacture, sale, or transportation of intoxicating liquors for beverage purposes." That was followed by a lengthy state-level ratification process, congressional passage of the Volstead Act and, finally, Prohibition enforcement starting in January 1920.

With Prohibition taking effect, Vallejo's 100 or so saloons joined their counterparts across the country in no longer selling liquor. At least, that's what they said for the record.

Sailors enjoyed their beers in a Lower Georgia Street saloon in late 1917, the year Congress initiated a ban on sale of liquor. Prohibition was enforced from early 1920 until late 1933—but that did not stop people from drinking. (*Jack Stiltz collection*)

Enforcement of Prohibition led to many arrests and penalties for bootlegging and other liquor-related crimes in Vallejo. Accounts of those crimes ran in newspapers throughout the years that Prohibition remained in force, before finally ending on Dec. 5, 1933. But enforcement was difficult given an ingrained Navy "liberty town" culture, and an attitude that Prohibition was a bad idea, maybe even a joke. If penalties were imposed, they tended to be light.

The Navy made repeated demands for a Vallejo "clean-up." One Mare Island commandant, Rear Adm. John Dayton, at one point threatened to close Vallejo to all sailors "unless vice conditions are cleaned up and the moral tone of the town changed within 30 days." The admiral's demands were mocked in a newspaper editorial that stated:

> We read about a Lily White or spotless town once and as we remember it the town was described as so sleepy that a man dropped dead in front of the post office on Monday and his body was not discovered until the following Thursday.

A January 1921 newspaper story told of the arrests of two Vallejo police officers for taking bribes from a bootlegger. One officer, jailed in Fairfield, managed to saw the bars on his cell and escape. The other officer pled guilty and was placed on probation for five years, on the condition that he return to his parents' ranch in Idaho.

A 1921 newspaper story dealt with an investigation into theft of 200 gallons of alcohol from the paint shop on Mare Island. A Navy lieutenant faced a court martial on a charge of arranging to sell the alcohol to bootleggers in San Francisco. The officer became a suspect because he acquired some large cans that could have been used to transport the alcohol. He was cleared after claiming that he was going to haul gasoline in the cans on a planned road trip.

A federal raid in 1932 resulted in the arrests of seven men, all with businesses in Vallejo's infamous Lower Georgia Street sailor district. Each was fined $100, but a citizens' delegation then urged city council members to cancel the business licenses held by the men. One delegation member, Guy Hale, went too far, saying, "If you gentlemen can't handle these matters, we will have to go to other sources." An irritated Mayor Fred Heegler snapped, "It ill becomes you to appear here and make a veiled threat of that kind." Hale quickly apologized.

During the Prohibition years there were small stills "all over town," according to Vallejo native Ray Bowman. That included one that his father, Al Bowman, had in his backyard in the early 1930s. Bowman said his father would take him along for night-time rides in the family car "to see a friend. He would see that friend—and then he would make a stop at another friend's house. Later, I realized he was delivering alky, in five-gallon cans."

Ed Burgle says his father, longtime Vallejo car dealer Gene Burgle, would put on "duck feeds" for his customers, and during Prohibition found an innovative way to get lots of the birds. Rancher friends had a still on a marshy island along the Napa River, just north of Vallejo, and would toss left-over mash from the still into the water. "The ducks would be eating all that grain, and they would pretty much be swimming in circles after a while," Burgle said. "He would row out and fill gunny sacks with drunk ducks, and then would put on these duck feeds."

Vallejo Yacht Club member Tom Ochs says that during Prohibition liquor could be smuggled by boat into an old clubhouse, built over the water. The liquor would be pulled up through a secret hatch, in a janitor's closet, that opened directly to the river. "And you could always tell when the stuff came in because some judge's car, or the mayor's car, or the police chief's car would be parked on the street in front of the club," Ochs says.

The day before the Dec. 5, 1933, end of the Prohibition era, the *Vallejo Times-Herald* editorialized about the need for responsibility, saying the chief trouble with the old-time saloon was that it "had precious little discretion. It sold, in most cases, to anyone who could lay a coin on the bar—to chronic drunkards, to spendthrifts, to flighty youngsters, and to men whose families were in want."

Another editorial ran in the newspaper the next day, as repeal took effect, again urging responsibility and also noting that Prohibition led to "no less than 200,000 speakeasies in the nation and, in a very short time, these formed the framework and the background for gangsterism and racketeering that have no equal in history."

More details on Prohibition in Vallejo are in my book, *Lower Georgia Street: California's Forgotten Barbary Coast*. Daniel Okrent's *Last Call: The Rise and Fall of Prohibition* is a great account of the Grand Experiment on a national level.

2

2018 Columns

Bill Stanford Served 36 Years as Vallejo's First Police Chief (Jan. 7, 2018)

William "Bill" Stanford, a Mare Island Naval Shipyard mechanic with no police experience, was named Vallejo's first police chief on April 4, 1900. But Stanford made up for his lack of experience with plenty of determination—he held the chief's job, through some very tough times, for nearly 36 years.

Vallejo trustees chose Stanford over 18 other applicants, and assigned him three patrolmen to police a town of about 7,000 residents. His new department, mandated by voters concerned about growing crime problems, replaced an outdated arrangement of a town marshal, two constables and a night watchman.

The 32-year-old Stanford promptly launched a clean-up campaign, but ran into opposition from operators of some of the town's saloons, gambling houses and bordellos—and even from some local officials.

Among Stanford's first targets was the Waldorf Saloon. The proprietor, W. R. Acock, had warned Stanford to stay out, but in late September 1900 the chief rushed to the bar when told that trouble was brewing there. When he tried to enter, Acock hit him on the head with the butt of his pistol. Stanford fired his gun but, blinded by blood from his head wound, missed Acock. Fined $200, Acock later tried unsuccessfully to revise the city charter to eliminate the new police department.

The city's clean-up efforts also included an ordinance giving Stanford authority to regulate retail liquor sales and to prevent games of chance in places where liquor was sold. However, that plan was vetoed in October 1900 by Mayor Joel A. Harvey.

The year ended with Stanford getting warrants that accused 31 people of illegal gambling at the Leader Saloon, at 225 Georgia St. The police chief also went after the Waldorf again, but the *Vallejo Evening Chronicle* said gamblers there had been tipped off by the county sheriff, George Savage, and "many of them took the train for San Francisco" to avoid arrest.

Vallejo's saloons remained a constant problem for Stanford. By 1906, the town's population had more than doubled, to about 16,000, and the number of bars was approaching 100. The chief got an assist from the Navy, which forced a reduction in the saloon count by threatening to decrease shipyard jobs.

Bill Stanford had no experience as a cop when he was named Vallejo's first police chief in 1900, but he made up for that with determination and wound up serving nearly thirty-six years as chief. (*Vallejo Naval and Historical Museum*)

The battle over vice heated up again in August 1910, with Stanford and Mayor J. F. Chappell facing grand jury questions about complaints that liquor was being sold in dance halls, gambling was flourishing and prostitutes had rented rooms above downtown stores. The chief and the mayor promised to take care of the problems. Also in 1910, Stanford helped to track down a murder suspect from Kentucky who had been hiding out in Vallejo.

Stanford had no reservations about street duty. In 1911, he was in a gunfight with a robbery suspect who he shot in the hip; and several months later got a burn mark on his ear from a bullet fired by a Canadian killer trying to avoid arrest.

By 1914, the number of Vallejo saloons was down to 45 and Stanford's department had tripled in size, to a dozen officers. But with the 1917 entry of the United States into World War I, thousands of sailors and Marines were sent to Mare Island and the Navy complained that police weren't doing enough to prevent vice. Stanford countered that the complaint was "unjust and absolutely unwarranted."

World War I ended on Nov. 11, 1918, and within a few months 1,500 Mare Island sailors were discharged. Vallejo quieted down and Stanford's workload decreased—but not for long. With Prohibition taking effect in January 1920, his officers joined in a long enforcement battle, making many arrests for bootlegging and other liquor-related crimes until Prohibition ended in late 1933.

The chief also had in-house problems during the Prohibition era. In early 1921, two of his officers were charged with taking bribes from a bootlegger; and in 1932 four officers resigned rather than face charges of taking bribes from brothel operators.

More demands for a Vallejo "clean-up" were made in early 1925 by the Mare Island commandant. Rear Adm. John Dayton complained about "wide-open gambling dens, bootleg joints, disorderly houses and trafficking in narcotics." At about the same time, Stanford was accused by one of his own officers, Arthur Clark, of failing to stop crime in the town.

Officer Clark, who had been raiding bootleg joints without the chief's sanction, was in turn accused of insubordination. During a stormy hearing on Clark's claims, a special investigator named many locations where "liquor and narcotics were sold and where gambling and prostitution took place," the *Vallejo Evening Chronicle* reported. The investigator also said Stanford was seen coming out of "the most prominent bootlegging establishment in Vallejo." Stanford denied being in the club.

During the hearing, the assistant city health officer testified that medical examinations of Vallejo prostitutes had been started in efforts to prevent venereal disease. That in turn led to arguments by Stanford that the city council and mayor had "tolerated" prostitution. Finally, Officer Clark resigned and the city council voted 2-1 to exonerate Chief Stanford and to declare Clark's charges "without basis or foundation of fact."

In April 1931, Chief Stanford was honored by the Police and Peace Officers' Journal of California for his long service—31 years at that point. A lengthy article in the journal included a glowing tribute from Thomas O'Hara, head of the Vallejo Chamber of Commerce, who praised Stanford for a record of honesty, efficiency and vigilance in keeping crime "at a minimum in our community."

On Feb. 1, 1936, Stanford, 68, retired with a pension of $125 a month, one-half his salary. His nearly 36 years of Vallejo service made him the longest-serving police chief in the nation at that time. He moved to Southern California, but returned from time to time to Vallejo. He died in a Glendale nursing home on May 1, 1964, at age 96.

Navy Jobbed Out Some Ship Work to Vallejo-side Shipyards (Feb. 4, 2018)

The Navy built more than 500 vessels on Mare Island over the years, but it wasn't the only shipyard on the Mare Island Strait. Several shipyards flourished in the late 1800s and early 1900s on the Vallejo side of the river, including one that built a Navy warship, the USS *Monadnock*.

The first known shipyard in Vallejo was Kimball's Ways, where Napa Street intersects with Curtola Parkway. That's dry land now but that wasn't the case in 1873 when Kimball built the Star of Vallejo and launched the 100-ton schooner into a much wider Napa River. How all that land was created between Curtola Parkway, once known as Maryland Street, and the current waterfront is a story for another day.

Many ships, ranging from schooners and ferryboats to tugs and scows were built or repaired at Kimball's Ways until it was sold in 1876. In the same time frame, *Vallejo Evening Chronicle* publisher Frank Leach helped to organize a cooperative shipbuilding association which built a 125-foot, three-masted schooner, the Joseph Perkins. The idea was to help find work for workers who had lost their jobs due to reduced Navy activity on Mare Island. The federal shipyard, which employed about 2,000 men in 1872, averaged only about 330 employees in 1876.

The plan for the shipbuilding association got strong endorsements from area newspapers. The San Francisco Bulletin commented that Vallejo had "greater facilities

USS *Monadnock* was built in one of Vallejo's early-day shipyards, which flourished in the late 1800s and early 1900s. It was the only warship built in Vallejo. (*Vallejo Naval and Historical Museum*)

for this business than any other place on the Pacific Coast. The trouble with Vallejo has long been that the people trust too much in the Navy Yard, when that institution should be an incident to the prosperity of the city."

Leach, encouraged by his success in starting the association, then established a shipyard between Maine and Pennsylvania streets on the Vallejo waterfront. In late 1875, financial problems resulted in the yard being taken over by the Vallejo Dock Co., whose directors included John Frisbie, Gen. Mariano Vallejo's son-in-law.

In 1874, shipbuilder Phineas Burgess got a contract to overhaul the Navy monitor Camanche, which had been berthed at Mare Island. The extensive work on the Camanche, by more than 70 men, won praise from the Navy and resulted in Burgess getting a contract to build the 263-foot, nearly 4,000-ton USS *Monadnock*.

The building ways for the *Monadnock* were located at the foot of Santa Clara Street near its intersection with Pennsylvania Street—like Kimball's Ways now dry land due to an extension of the Vallejo waterfront. As many as 100 men worked on the ship starting in November 1875, but because of delayed congressional funding the *Monadnock* wasn't launched until September 1883. But the private shipyard lacked funds for completing the ship, and the Navy commandeered it. After being towed to Mare Island, the ship was slowly completed—at a cost of $3 million—and finally commissioned in February 1896. The *Monadnock* has the dubious distinction of holding the Navy record for time between start and completion of one ship, according to Vallejo historian Thomas Lucy. The ship got to sea just in time for the Spanish-American War—for which she was already outdated.

Another Vallejo shipyard was established by A. K. Irving and William Brown at the intersection of Marin and Maryland streets—another location that's no longer riverfront. Many scow schooners were built there and at the nearby Vallejo Dock Co. in the mid-1870s. The schooners were among more than 600 such vessels, ranging in length from 44 to 89 feet, built around the San Francisco Bay area and used to haul all sorts of cargo. One scow schooner remains, the *Alma*, in the National Maritime collection in San Francisco.

The Aden Brothers Shipyard, also known as Adenville, was founded in the early 1880s at the former Vallejo Dock Co. location. Three acres of ground were occupied by warehouses, wharves, a lumber yard and mill. The yard built ships of various sizes and also handled overhauls of vessels. The Adens owned the steamers Sunol and Hope along with 20 schooners of varying sizes. The shipyard was closed in about 1910.

The Standard Launch Co. also was located in Vallejo, at the intersection of Rice and Fifth streets. Like several other yards, it's also now an inland location—farther away from the Napa River than any of the other yards, as a result of a massive project in the early 1900s to deepen the main Mare Island Strait channel and use the dredged mud to create low-lying waterfront land. Standard, owned by William Nutz, built launches ranging in length from 23 to 48 feet. The company's known years of operation were from 1901 through 1905.

Besides the private shipyards along the Maryland Street shoreline, there were nearby bars and brothels. A 1901 map of the area shows a "ladies' boarding house" one block away, on Pennsylvania Street between Sonoma Boulevard and Sutter Street. On the same block there was a dance hall and saloon. A block to the west, near Pennsylvania and Marin streets, the "This is It" club catered to shipyard workers and sailors.

Most of the details for this column came from Thomas Lucy's "Early Shipbuilding and Repair in Vallejo" article, published in the December 1990 edition of the *Solano Historian*. Additional information can be found in Frank Leach's "Recollections of a Newspaperman" in *Sidewheelers to Nuclear Power* by Vallejo and Mare Island historians Sue Lemmon and Ernie Wichels; and in Arnold Lott's *A Long Line of Ships*.

Projects Narrowed River, Expanded Mare Island and Vallejo Shorelines (Feb. 18, 2018)

Efforts to extend the shorelines of Mare Island and Vallejo, narrowing the Napa River channel between them, date to the earliest days of the city and the Navy's first West Coast shipyard. Old navigation charts show the Navy, which began operating Mare Island Naval Shipyard in 1854, quickly filled in a strip of marshland along the river and constructed a seawall or quay where ships could tie up.

Expansion of Mare Island to meet navy demands continued for more than a century, resulting in the shipyard increasing from less than 1,000 acres to its estimated 5,600 acres today. The new land was formed all the way around the island mainly by dredged mud from Mare Island Strait, the renamed stretch of river between the island and Vallejo, and by fill that was imported or obtained by digging into original higher ground on the island. Some of the new land has had little or no development and is designated as marsh or tidal land on current maps. But at least half of all that new land has streets and roads and was used for all types of Navy shipyard activity.

On the Vallejo side, expansion into the Mare Island Strait added nearly 500 acres along the waterfront, from near the Highway 37 bridge on the north side of Vallejo to the old Sperry Mill site in South Vallejo.

One ambitious project filled in a wide section of river that once separated Vallejo from South Vallejo. The new land was formed in the early 1900s by establishing a barrier that ran straight from what's now the city boat ramp almost to Lemon Street in

South Vallejo. Mud dredged from the river on the west side of the barrier, or bulwark, was then pumped into what once had been navigable water and tideland on the other side. The dredge-and-fill process that began on a large scale in 1913 took several years, creating more land and more direct road links between the two communities. Present-day Sonoma Boulevard between Curtola Parkway and Lemon Street would not exist without this project. The same goes for the city's sewage treatment plant, the Kiewit Pacific Co. yard on the river, and many other businesses. Without all the fill, you could anchor a boat at the present-day location of Anchor Self Storage on Sonoma Boulevard. Along what's now Curtola Parkway, the north side of this fill project, ship-builders once launched ships and boats. The river spread as far east as Fifth Street, where it turned into a marshy connection to Lake Dalwigk. On the south side, the railroad tracks that cross Fifth Street near Solano Avenue once ran along the water's edge into South Vallejo.

More acreage was added to Vallejo's shoreline in the 1960s as part of a massive redevelopment project that resulted in Vallejo's entire Lower Georgia Street business district being bulldozed. Many longtime Vallejoans can remember walking out on a pier over tideland to board ferries that ran to Mare Island. That tideland is now the seawall area where people can park cars, take a ferryboat to San Francisco, have a drink or dine out, or go for a stroll. Before redevelopment, the original Vallejo Yacht Club building stood in the same location as the current building—but on pilings over tideland. At high tide, Prohibition-era bootleggers could row boats under the club and sneak in booze through a secret hatch. Much of the fill dirt for this waterfront extension came from Vallejo's historic York Street Hill—the site of California's Capitol in 1852 and 1853. The hill was scraped flat and trucked to the nearby riverfront.

Besides adding land, proponents of the shoreline-extending projects said the resulting narrowed river channel would speed up water flow and prevent silt build-up—but periodic dredging is still necessary.

Besides the shoreline work, nearly 500 acres of usable land were formed by levees and fill in a marshy area where Larwin Plaza, now Vallejo Plaza, was built in 1960, along Sonoma Boulevard on the north side of Vallejo. White Slough, which flows into the Napa River, is on the edge of this shopping center. Traces of the marsh once extended nearly to Tennessee Street, several blocks away. There's a similar situation near Lake Dalwigk on the south side of Vallejo, where many homeowners in nearby neighborhoods must have sump pumps in basements. Old maps show marshy areas and a small creek extending south and east toward Magazine Street. Sump pumps also are needed in other areas, including parts of Vallejo's historic downtown, due to underground streams, springs, subsurface infiltration of river water and other sources.

The history is interesting, but things get even more interesting given the potential for rising sea levels caused by melting glaciers and ice sheets. Vallejo is part of a new study by a group called Resilient by Design to determine what residents consider most important to protect from the sea rise. There's an interactive risk-zone map at http://sealevel.climatecentral.org/maps that shows the impact of rising levels that could reach three to five feet a century from now. Without continued efforts to prevent flooding, much of the expanded Vallejo and Mare Island shorelines, along with part of Highway 37, would be threatened. The flood controls that already exist includes a network of buried 9-foot diameter pipes that can carry storm water away from town and into the river.

An image provided by Cecil Howell, landscape architect on the Resilient by Design team, shows some of the historic water and marsh areas. "This kind of historical mapping can give us insights into how the landscape got to be the way it is now," Howell says.

We can see places where people's basements get flooded because they once were tidal marshes. Many of the same areas that were filled in are most threatened by sea level rise, too. So maps like this can help us think about where we might let nature and water back into the landscape, and how we can better protect the community, the city, and the infrastructure that helps it run.

Vallejo Area Has Its Share of Sunken Ship Stories (March 18, 2018)

The Vallejo area has its share of sunken ship stories, including a navy destroyer rusting away in Napa River mud north of town and the submerged hulk of a massive ferryboat, once used to haul entire trains, to the south in Carquinez Strait.

Elsewhere along the strait, the river and adjacent sloughs, there are more hulks, some abandoned and decaying, others burned to their waterlines by fire. All once were part of a wide-ranging network of waterborne commercial and military activity.

A kayaker paddles around the hull of an old navy destroyer rusting away in the Napa River just north of Vallejo. It is one of numerous hulks that exist in the river, nearby sloughs, and the Carquinez Strait. (*Vallejo Naval and Historical Museum*)

There are many figurative reefs and shoals for anyone claiming to have a full list of the wrecks in Vallejo-area waters. The safer course is to describe better-known ones, starting with the hulk of the 314-foot USS *Corry*, located about three miles north of the Highway 37 bridge on the east side of the Napa River.

The *Corry* (DD-334), built in San Francisco and commissioned in 1921 at Mare Island Naval Shipyard, was one of 273 destroyers known as "four-pipers" for their distinctive smokestacks. These fast, flush-deck ships were the standard U.S. destroyers in World War I—but the war was over when the *Corry* was commissioned. After nine years of peacetime service in the fleet, the ship was stripped and sold for scrap.

How the *Corry* ended up along a Napa River levee bank isn't clear. One explanation years ago from Vallejo rancher Severus "Toots" Mini was that the hulk was used to shore up the levee. The *Corry* is one of the last remaining "four pipers"—what's left of it after nearly 90 years in the mud.

Across the river, the hulk of an 85-foot military freight hauler, designated FS (Freight Ship) 485, is in Dutchman Slough, which flows into the Napa River a few hundred yards north of the Highway 37 bridge. FS 485 hauled freight in the Aleutian Islands during WWII, and then wound up in the San Francisco area. The late Bill Bird, who owned the Napa-Val Fishing Resort near the bridge, said in a 1974 interview that the ship was towed to Napa-Val in the early 1960s and abandoned. The resort is gone, but the deteriorating FS 485 is still there. It's a regular stop for local kayak tours organized by Steve Souza.

Another old wreck is located on the Napa River at Cuttings Wharf, about 10 miles by water north of Vallejo: the SS *Cabrillo*, a 194-foot, 1,200-passenger steamship that carried passengers from Los Angeles to Catalina Island from 1904 to the early 1940s. The luxurious ship, nicknamed the "Queen of the South Coast," was featured in *The Real Glory*, a 1939 film starring Gary Cooper, David Niven and Broderick Crawford. During World War II, the *Cabrillo* became an Army troopship and ferried thousands of soldiers to various San Francisco Bay area points. The ship was towed in about 1950 to Cuttings Wharf. Plans by then-owner Chuck Moore to use it as a restaurant, nightclub and hotel never materialized, and over the years it was completely stripped. All that's left is its rotting hull.

At the California Maritime Academy, in South Vallejo's Morrow Cove on the Carquinez Strait, a buoy marks the submerged hulk of the SS Contra Costa, a 433-foot rail ferry described as the largest of its kind when launched in 1914. The ferry wasn't needed after a railroad bridge between Martinez and Benicia was completed in 1930. The Contra Costa then was anchored in Morrow Cove and used as a fishing resort. After the CMA moved to the cove in the early 1940s, the big ship, which had become a safety hazard, was burned to the waterline and the hulk was dynamited.

Also in Morrow Cove for many years was the Bangor, a four-masted, 165-foot schooner that made many ocean voyages after being launched in 1891. In 1927, her sailing days over, the Bangor was used as a fender to protect the center span of the bridge being constructed between Vallejo and Crockett. When the bridge over the Carquinez Strait was completed, the beat-up Bangor was towed to the nearby cove and abandoned. The Bangor was later burned, and dirt fill at CMA now covers its location.

Going up the Carquinez Strait, there are many sunken ship sites. They include wreckage of the 208-foot Garden City, visible from the fishing pier at Eckley, between

Crockett and Port Costa. The sidewheeler, built in 1879, was last used as a ferry on a Vallejo-Crockett run that ended in 1929. The Garden City was still afloat in 1983 when it was destroyed by a fire set by an arsonist.

The mud-covered remains of the *Stamboul*, a 106-foot whaler built in Massachusetts in 1843, are located about 120 yards off the shoreline at the foot of 12th Street in Benicia, within Matthew Turner Shipyard Park. Turner constructed 228 vessels over 33 years—more than any other single shipbuilder in North America. Two-thirds of those ships were launched at his Benicia shipyard, where the *Stamboul* was grounded for use as a work platform.

Across the strait, the hull of the 217-foot schooner *Forester*, clearly visible at low tide, is located close to shore a half-mile west of the Martinez marina. The ship ended up in Martinez in the early 1930s after about 30 years in the lumber trade and a final use— just like the Bangor—as a Carquinez Bridge fender. The four-masted *Forester*, launched in 1900, was destroyed by fire in 1975.

There are many more wrecks sites if you head upriver or toward the Pacific Ocean. That includes a dozen wrecks just between Benicia and the point that Carquinez Strait flows into San Pablo Bay, according to a 1997 state Lands Commission report. The ships aren't named in the report, but are believed to include those Carquinez Strait wrecks named in this column. For some good reading on coastal wrecks, read *Shipwrecks at the Golden Gate*, a 1989 book by James Delgado and Stephen Haller.

Vallejo Had Its Own Quicksilver Mining District (April 1, 2018)

California's fabulous Mother Lode was being mined for fortunes in gold when an enterprising prospector discovered cinnabar, a source of mercury needed to extract gold from ore, in the early 1850s just north of Vallejo on Sulphur Springs Mountain.

Over time, 10 known mercury mines were opened on the mountain. Demand for mercury, a toxic liquid metal also known as quicksilver, continued as the Gold Rush was followed by Nevada's Comstock Lode mining boom. After that, mining was sporadic, with gaps of many years—but limited activity continued into the 1960s.

Sulphur Springs Mountain runs roughly parallel to Columbus Parkway between Interstate 80 and Lake Herman Road on Vallejo's east side. With its 1,112-foot north summit near I-80, listed on some old maps as Mt. St. John, and a 970-foot peak nearly four miles to the southeast near Lake Herman, Sulphur Springs Mountain may have a singular name but it's more like a small mountain range. Between the two peaks, there are lower-elevation hills directly above Blue Rock Springs.

Some of the old shafts remained open for years after mining activity had stopped—and they were a danger to hikers until their adits, or entrances, were filled in. My brothers, Tim and Mike, and I were among many local youngsters who ventured into those mines and fortunately weren't hurt—but others weren't so lucky. In 1953 an 11-year-old boy fell down a 35-foot-deep shaft, breaking an arm and a rib. A bulldozer filled the entrance with dirt, and several sticks of dynamite were used to close a nearby shaft that the bulldozer couldn't reach. In 1959, another mine opening was closed after a 12-year-old boy broke his back in a fall down a 20-foot-deep shaft. A front-page story in the *Vallejo Times-Herald* warned parents to instruct their children to stay away from the mines.

John Neate, an Englishman who came to California in 1850 and ran a cement plant in Benicia, is credited with making the first discovery of cinnabar on Sulphur Springs Mountain in 1852. Actual mining didn't start until the late 1860s on John Brownlie's ranch, on a ridge above what's now the big Syar Industries quarry. Two Brownlie mines produced quicksilver worth more than $30,000 before closing in the mid-1870s.

Neate kept on prospecting, making another discovery in 1873 on the north end of Sulphur Springs Mountain that led to formation of the St. John Quicksilver Mining Co. By 1880, as many as 150 miners were working 600 feet below ground there and more than 11,000 flasks of quicksilver, each holding 70 pounds of mercury, had been produced. But low quicksilver prices forced the mine to close that year, and it was idle until 1899. The mine closed down again in 1909, reopened in 1914, and then closed again in 1923 due to failing profits. At that point, two St. John mines had shafts and tunnels that ran for thousands of feet. The mines opened again for short periods during World War II and in the late 1950s. Now the mineshafts are flooded, the buildings are gone, and only a crumbling brick kiln and piles of mine tailings remain.

In late 1874, T. M. Loup discovered cinnabar on the east side of Sulphur Springs Mountain, on Daniel Hastings' ranch on Sky Valley Road, just off Lake Herman Road. There were two Hastings mines, including one that extended into the source of Blue Rock Springs in 1929, diverting water through the shaft into Lake Herman. The diversion, at a rate of three million

The long-closed St. John's Mine, located near the top of Sulphur Springs Mountain on the north side of Vallejo, was one of ten known quicksilver mines on the mountain. Part of a kiln remains, but the buildings are gone. (*Vallejo Naval and Historical Museum*)

gallons a day, dried up Blue Rock Springs and caused hundreds of shrubs and trees to die there. The springs began flowing again following a legal battle and a 1930 court order to close the mine. Some ruins of brick furnaces and a chimney remain there now.

Two more mercury mines were located on the south slope of Sulphur Springs Mountain, on Tony Borges' ranchland along Lake Herman Road. There was mining activity at that site in the mid-1960s. Other quicksilver mines were dug on an 816-foot-high hill above Blue Rock Springs Park and close to Columbus Parkway just north of the park. It's not clear who developed those mines.

A federal Department of Mineral Resources report states that all the mines on Sulphur Springs Mountain produced more than 17,000 flasks of mercury, most of it from the St. John site, and there's potential for more mining "under favorable economic conditions."

However, a 2009 California Regional Water Quality Control Board report raised concerns about the old St. John mine, noting that there were mine tailings, some with high mercury concentrations, on the steep hillside that weren't adequately protected against erosion. The agency's main concern was the potential for mercury pollution getting into Rindler Creek, which runs off the mountain, and eventually reaching Vallejo's Lake Chabot next to Six Flags Discovery Kingdom. The report also mentions the Hastings Mine site, but says there's a low risk of any mercury waste getting into a creek that drains into Lake Herman.

More information on the local mining activity is available at the Vallejo Naval and Historical Museum. Also, here's a link to a site with more details on the 10 known Sulphur Springs Mountain mines, plus an 11th mine that's on another hill along I-80, near the Highway 12 junction at Cordelia. This site provides topo maps and latitude-longitude:

https://westernmininghistory.com/mine_county/california/solano/

And another link for hikers: http://www.peakbagger.com/peak.aspx?pid=53601

Vallejo's Urban Renewal Effort Had Mixed Results
(April 15, 2018)

Vallejo leaders, joining in the grand schemes of other U.S. cities during the nation's urban renewal era a half-century ago, began by bulldozing 24 blocks of the city's original downtown and adjacent side streets. It was a big deal for this city—and one that didn't live up to expectations.

Congress launched urban renewal with the Housing Act of 1949. That legislation and amendments in the 1950s provided federal funding to cover two-thirds of many redevelopment costs, and Vallejo followed up in 1956 by creating a redevelopment agency, headed by Jim Richardson, for its Marina Vista project. Demolition began in 1961, and by 1970 more than 500 structures had been torn down in an area covering about 100 acres. Another 25 acres were added by building a seawall in what had been a tidal zone and then backfilling earth behind the new wall. The dirt, about 1 million cubic yards, came from York Street hill, on which the Capitol of California once stood. The hill was bulldozed flat, lowered by about 40 feet.

Among the demolished structures were all the old buildings in the once-notorious Lower Georgia Street sailor district—no big loss, as far as many Vallejoans were concerned. But some landmarks also were torn down, including a Navy YMCA building built in 1903 in hopes of giving sailors a better option than the dive bars and boarding houses on Lower Georgia Street; the Astor House, originally the Metropolitan House, built in 1859; the Vallejo Women's Club, originally designed as a YWCA by famed architect Julia Morgan; the 8-story Georgian Hotel; a Bank of America branch; and the city's beautiful Andrew Carnegie Library—the final and most controversial target of redevelopment, torn down in 1970. The entire 24-block area had been given a "blighted" label, to help make the case to the federal government that the property was deteriorated badly enough to qualify for federal funding.

Workers made a grim discovery when the Naval Base Cafe building at 147 Georgia St. was demolished in 1962: a dungeon-like basement, with thick brick walls, barred windows and what appeared to be individual cells. The structure was built in 1870 on the southwest corner of Georgia and Santa Clara streets by early-day Vallejo businessman Philip Bernard Lynch.

When the building was torn down, Lynch's grandson, then-Superior Court Judge Philip Lynch, recalled that the basement was used as a storeroom. He wasn't certain that it was used as a jail but agreed that it could have been after the Lynch family sold the property, prior to the war years. Vallejo native and just-retired Superior Court Judge Paul Beeman recently recounted a story he heard from his father: During World War II, military police used the dungeon as a temporary brig for sailors and Marines who had been picked up for causing trouble in bars or on the street. Locked gates and bars were

Vallejo bulldozed twenty-four blocks of the city's original downtown in a major urban renewal project. One citizen said the area looked like "it was hit by The Bomb." (*Vallejo Naval and Historical Museum*)

installed, and straw was tossed on the floor. There were no toilets and no water. "It was almost as bad as water-boarding," Beeman said.

Before construction of any new buildings in the bulldozed redevelopment area, a *Times-Herald* column quoted one citizen as saying, "The place looks like it was hit by The Bomb." Similar cynical descriptions of "big bulldozer" sites included "Hiroshima Flats" in St. Louis and "Ragweed Acres" in Detroit. In Buffalo, a chamber of commerce staffer said a cleared-off 29-block area might be mistaken for an airplane landing strip.

By the mid-1970s, a new 60,000-square-foot city hall, public library and post office had been built in what once was the heart of Vallejo's Lower Georgia Street district. Commercial projects and apartment construction also had started. Combined redevelopment costs at that point exceeded $20 million, covered mainly by federal funds and local bond revenue.

But there were ominous signs, including banking as the primary commercial use and only a limited number of retail outlets to draw shoppers into the area. Of the more than 600 new apartment units constructed by 1970, nearly two-thirds were designated for low-income families. Some big retailers decided against buying building sites that included new utilities and other improvements and instead relocated to the new Larwin Plaza shopping center, which had been built in the early 1960s north of the old downtown. By the 1980s, many businesses in the downtown area just outside the redevelopment zone had closed, unable to compete against Larwin Plaza and other malls being built closer to freeways.

Redevelopment had many advocates—among them Luther Gibson, publisher of the morning *Vallejo Times-Herald* and afternoon *Vallejo News-Chronicle*. Gibson's power base and political connections extended from Sacramento, where he served as a leading Democratic state senator, to Washington, D.C., the source of federal redevelopment dollars. But redevelopment also had its critics. They included the late Jack Burstein, who started practicing law in Vallejo in the mid-1950s, in an office on Georgia Street, a half block from the Lower Georgia district. Burstein says his first impression of the Lower Georgia district was "a place that was buzzing all the time. What a pity to tear it down. That was the worst tragedy that ever happened to Vallejo, in my opinion, because you had thriving traffic going back and forth, and it became dead because of so-called redevelopment."

Extensive files on Vallejo's redevelopment project are in the Vallejo Naval and Historical Museum. Also, here's a link to a good overview of urban renewal in America, by historian and author Jon C. Teaford: https://pdfs.semanticscholar. org/4ef3/28b64fdb97357674725324ccc7380d8220ca.pdf

The abstract reads:

The federal urban renewal program created by Title I of the Housing Act of 1949 fell short of expectations and spawned an army of critics. Originally the program had promised a great deal to a variety of interests, but it could not accommodate all of its early supporters. Social reformers and low-rent housing advocates were among the first backers who found it wanting. By the early 1960s, the foes of big government and critics of prevailing planning orthodoxies were exploiting the program's shortcomings to further their own agendas.

The impact of urban renewal, however, was never as great as some observers assumed, and its physical legacy was limited. Yet its record did influence later federal revitalization programs that granted local authorities greater flexibility and emphasized rehabilitation and the urban context. Moreover, it called into question the efficacy of planning panaceas and federal dollars in solving urban problems.

Lower Georgia Street Dungeon Discovery Prompted Lots of Speculation (June 24, 2018)

Fable can get mixed up with fact when it comes to stories about Vallejo's once-notorious Lower Georgia Street sailor district—especially the tales of an underground network of tunnels that could have been used for all sorts of nefarious purposes.

Tunnel tales have circulated for years, fueled by a grim discovery a half-century ago when the Naval Base Cafe building at 147 Georgia St. was torn down. During the demolition, as part of Vallejo's massive downtown redevelopment project, workers found a dungeon-like basement that was secure as any prison, with thick brick walls and barred windows.

The building was constructed in 1870 on the southwest corner of Georgia and Santa Clara streets by early-day Vallejo merchant Philip Bernard Lynch. A native of Ireland who came to Vallejo in 1858, he ran a grocery store on the main floor and lived with his family on the second floor. A former city post office stands there now.

When the 1870 building was torn down in 1962, Lynch's grandson, then-Superior Court Judge Philip Lynch, recalled that part of the basement was used as a storeroom for the grocery store. He wasn't certain that it was ever used as a jail but agreed that it could have been after the Lynch family sold the property, prior to World War II.

Other ideas ranged from possible to improbable: the Lynch building was constructed on an older foundation that could have been the city's first jail; the basement was once a lock-up for shanghaied sailors; or it was a Spanish prison. There's no proof for any of those suggestions, especially the Spanish prison. Explorers from Spain came close to this

Tales of tunnels beneath Vallejo's infamous Lower Georgia Street area have circulated for years, fueled by the 1962 discovery of what appeared to be an underground jail. (*Vallejo Naval and Historical Museum*)

area in the 1770s, but didn't stop. About 60 years later, Mariano Vallejo passed by the bare land that would later become the city bearing his name—and Spain was out of the picture. In the 1830s, this was part of Mexico's northern frontier, and Mariano Vallejo's building activity was in Sonoma, not here.

The most plausible explanation comes from recently retired Superior Court Judge Paul Beeman, who says his father, who came here in the 1920s, told him that during World War II military police needed a temporary brig for sailors and Marines who had been causing trouble in bars or on the street. They would be held there until the end of the night and then loaded onto a bus and taken to Mare Island.

Beeman said the brig was created by breaking through the basement walls of the Lynch building into an old, brick-lined sewer system that hadn't been used for years. Locked gates and bars were installed, and straw was tossed on the floor. There were no toilets and no water. "It was almost as bad as water-boarding," Beeman said.

Beeman's description fits in with what Louis Orantes saw as an employee of Bayshore Wreckers, which had a demolition contract for part of the downtown area in the 1960s. Orantes recalls going to work sites on Lower Georgia Street and seeing the old brick sewer lines and a couple of tunnels, all big enough to walk in.

"The tunnels were there—I saw them," Orantes says. "But I don't know who they belonged to or where they led to. I wish I had taken some pictures." He adds that one tunnel ran from what had been a building basement into Georgia Street, near the Sacramento Street intersection, but he couldn't see whether it went under the street to the other side. Co-workers might have explored the tunnel "but they're all gone now, all dead," Orantes said.

Other stories of tunnels in the Lower Georgia Street area include one told by Rudy Peretto Sr., a longtime Vallejo police officer who spent many hours at various Lower Georgia demolition sites, hunting for coins, bottles and anything else that was collectible. Rudy Peretto Jr. says his father told him there were tunnels that served as escape routes from basement gambling halls during the wide-open WWII period "so people could get out of there if the police showed up."

Ted Correy says he also heard stories about tunnels under Georgia Street from his father, Tom "Tux" Correy, who had the Golden West Café, a bar at 241 Georgia St. "They had all sorts of stuff below Georgia Street," Correy says. "I heard there was a tunnel that went to the Bank of America (on the corner of Georgia and Sacramento streets), but I never saw it. That was the bank for the Lower Georgia Street bars."

Dennis Sullivan, a retired Vallejo policeman whose first beat covered Lower Georgia Street, has a similar story about tunnels under gambling joints. Sullivan says he heard of one that led to Indian Alley, behind 124 Georgia St., the location of Dopey Norman's, a bar and gambling joint run by Norman Reinburg during WWII. But Sullivan adds he never actually saw the tunnel.

Other longtime Vallejoans say they too have heard varying versions of the tunnel stories. It's no surprise that those stories keep popping up. As described in my book, *Lower Georgia Street: California's Forgotten Barbary Coast*, the area was a hub of illicit activity. During WWII, there were about three dozen gambling locations and two dozen houses of prostitution. In earlier years, that same activity persisted although on a smaller scale. It's likely that operators of such businesses tried to find ways to prevent their customers from being arrested in police raids.

But first-hand information is limited, and there aren't any known photographs like those taken in 1962 during demolition of the old Lynch building. Adding to the difficulty of determining the extent of the tunnels was the redevelopment-era bulldozing of the entire Lower Georgia area. We're left with a few facts, fading memories—and more Vallejo mysteries.

Old Stories Tell of Brief Vallejo Stay by Future Duchess (Aug. 19, 2018)

Stories about Wallis Warfield Simpson living in Vallejo, long before she became the duchess of Windsor, have circulated for years, without much detail. Based on a fresh review of old military-related records and reports dealing with her first husband, career Navy officer Earl Winfield "Win" Spencer Jr., it looks like Wallis' stay in Vallejo was brief—no more than six weeks in the summer of 1920 while Spencer's ship was at Mare Island Naval Shipyard.

The numerous Wallis-slept-here tales vary, but most have one thing in common: Wallis and Win stayed in the Collins Apartments, now called the duchess of Windsor Apartments, at 524 Georgia St. The 3-story, Mission Revival-style building, built in 1907, was one of the best apartment houses in town.

Among the stories is one from Vallejo resident Wally Josephs. Wally, now 96, says he spent part of his childhood living with his mother, Bertha Josephs, in the Collins Apartments and she told him their first-floor apartment was the same one occupied by the future duchess a year before he was born. The *Times-Herald*'s Marion Devlin had similar information in a column she wrote years ago after interviewing Wally.

The duchess of Windsor was a long way from British royalty when she was married to a U.S. Navy officer and may have stayed briefly in a Vallejo apartment while his ship was tied up at Mare Island Naval Shipyard. (*Vallejo Naval and Historical Museum*)

Patti Hewitt Seymour says that during the 1960s she often visited her grandmother, Julia Moore, who lived at the Collins Apartments and would hear tales of how "royalty used to live here."

Vallejo historian Ernie Wichels also mentioned the Collins Apartments as a temporary home for Wallis, for whom Edward VIII gave up the throne of England, becoming the Duke of Windsor. In a *Times-Herald* column, Wichels described the Spencers' brief stay here as Vallejo's "marginal brush with history."

While most of the stories are similar, one version that ran in the Dec. 8, 1936, *Vallejo Evening Chronicle*, as the marriage plans of Wallis and Edward were making worldwide headlines, mentioned "unverified reports" that the Spencers lived at 33 Santa Paula Way in Vallejo for a few months in 1920. But that story fell apart a week later when a local contractor, Thomas Ward, informed the newspaper that he built the first house at that address in 1927.

The duchess of Windsor, interviewed in 1959 by a *San Francisco Chronicle* reporter while on a cross-country U.S. tour that included the San Francisco Bay area, was quoted as saying, "I visited Northern California a lifetime ago in 1920 but the Duke has never been there; I think he will love it." But the duchess didn't go into any details about her 1920 visit.

Old editions of the Army and Navy Register and other reports on Navy personnel assignments and ship movements show that Spencer was ordered in early May 1920 to duty aboard the USS *Aroostook*, a San Diego-based seaplane tender whose captain was Henry Mustin. Spencer, a lieutenant commander at the time, and Mustin had strong ties that went beyond their careers as pioneer Navy aviators. Wallis was the cousin of Mustin's spouse, Corinne DeForest Montague, and the Mustins had played match-makers by introducing Win and Wallis in April 1916.

By early July the *Aroostook* was tied up at Mare Island Naval Shipyard for work that took about six weeks. There are no city directories or other records to confirm a stay by the Spencers for that time at the Collins Apartments. Absent hard proof, it's an assumption based on the Navy-related files, stories of longtime Vallejoans and the common practice for married Navy couples to find nearby housing during ship repair periods. Also, Wallis had friends in the area, including San Francisco socialite Jane Selby Hayne. Just before Spencer got his orders to the *Aroostook*, Wallis had spent two weeks as Hayne's guest at a Pebble Beach lodge.

By mid-August 1920, Wallis was in Coronado, the *Aroostook*'s repairs were completed and the ship headed back to San Diego. That ended the only time that Spencer's Navy duties would have kept him at Mare Island long enough to warrant an apartment in Vallejo. Prior to that, following his Naval Academy graduation in 1910, he had assignments in Squantum, Mass., Pensacola, Fla., and San Diego.

After leaving the *Aroostook* in October 1920, he was reassigned to Pensacola. A year later, he transferred to the Navy's Bureau of Aeronautics in Washington, D.C. Wallis joined him, but left because of his heavy drinking and abuse. In December 1922 Spencer, separated from his wife and bored with his desk job, was given command of the USS *Pampanga*, a gunboat that patrolled the war-torn Canton Delta in China.

Wallis stayed in the nation's capital, had a short-lived affair with an Argentine diplomat, Felipe Espil, and then went to Paris in January 1924 with her cousin Corinne Mustin. Returning home, she found letters from Spencer begging her to come to China.

A nostalgic Wallis boarded the troop ship *Chaumont* in July 1924 in Norfolk, Va., and arrived in Manila a month later. She then boarded another ship and reached Hong Kong on Sept. 7. Wallis spent a year in Asia, mostly on her own or with friends after the reconciliation attempt failed. Wallis was coping with health problems when she returned to the U.S. in 1925. After arriving by ship in Seattle, she was joined by a sympathetic Spencer on a cross-country train ride to Chicago. In her 1956 memoir *The Heart Has Its Reasons*, she says they never met again. Their divorce was finalized in December 1927. Spencer remained in the Navy, retiring in 1939. He was in his fourth marriage when he died at age 61 in Coronado in 1950.

Wallis married shipping executive Ernest Aldrich Simpson in 1928. Living in London, she met Edward, Prince of Wales, in 1931 and became his mistress in 1934. Amid scandal, Edward ascended to the throne in January 1936. Determined to marry Wallis, he signed abdication documents the following December. Wallis' divorce from Simpson was finalized in May 1937, and she married Edward a month later in France. Author Michael Bloch, in *The Duchess of Windsor*, described her as a victim of her own ambition, who "experienced the ultimate fairy tale, becoming the adored favourite of the most glamorous bachelor of his time. The idyll went wrong when, ignoring her pleas, he threw up his position to spend the rest of his life with her." A recluse following Edward's death in 1972, she died at age 89 in her Paris home on April 24, 1986, and was buried next to Edward in the Royal Burial Ground near Windsor Castle.

A Tale of Two Lighthouses (Sept. 16, 2018)

This column was prompted by a recent flurry of Facebook posts about two lighthouses that once existed at the mouth of the Mare Island Strait, where it flows into the Carquinez Strait and San Pablo Bay. Their beacons and fog signals guided mariners through these often-hazardous waters for nearly 80 years.

The first lighthouse was built on the south end of Mare Island in 1873 and was demolished in the 1930s. The second lighthouse, a three-story, 28-room structure built offshore in 1909 at the end of a long Vallejo-side jetty, survived an improbable barge ride after its 1951 deactivation and now is at a marina two miles up Carquinez Strait.

The Mare Island Lighthouse was a combination 75-foot-high tower and two-story, Victorian-style home that was considered one of the most attractive lighthouses in the San Francisco Bay area. It was in service for 44 years, until its 1917 deactivation, and for 35 of those years its keeper was Kate Coffee McDougal, widow of Charles McDougal, a Navy commander in charge of the federal Lighthouse Service's stations along the California coast.

Kate McDougal got the Mare Island Lighthouse assignment after her husband drowned on March 28, 1881, while trying to go ashore at Cape Mendocino. He had arrived in the tender Manzanita, which anchored off the dangerous cape, and boarded a surf boat to visit lighthouse keepers stationed there. The surf boat capsized in heavy breakers and McDougal, 44, went under, weighed down by a money belt filled with gold coins, the keepers' pay. Two other men also drowned. His widow was left with a $50 monthly pension and four children to raise. When the first Mare Island Lighthouse keeper, Theresa Watson, decided to resign, Kate McDougal was offered her $800-a-year job.

Vallejo and Mare Island once had two lighthouses at the mouth of the Mare Island Strait. One was demolished, but the other lighthouse survived an improbable barge ride to a new location. (*Gordon Shaffer*)

While her station was a lonely outpost, the new keeper had close ties to Mare Island. Prior to his lighthouse duties, Cmdr. McDougal commanded many Navy ships, including the USS Camanche, stationed from time to time at Mare Island. He also had three years of Mare Island duty dealing with explosive ordnance, and was the son of a retired rear-admiral and former shipyard commandant, David Stockton McDougal.

There were many efforts to make life easier for Kate McDougal, including a telephone the first Christmas season after her husband's death. That was provided by a Navy officer on Mare Island related to Alexander Graham Bell, who had invented the telephone a few years earlier. The officer and some workmen put up poles and ran a phone line to the lighthouse. Other improvements were made over the years, including a new barn and shed in 1888, and hot water, a bathroom and a landing wharf in 1892. She also had a horse and buggy.

Citing poor health, Kate McDougal resigned as keeper about a month before the official July 1, 1917, closure of the lighthouse. She stayed here for the rest of her life, dying on Sept. 11, 1932, at age 90 at the home of her daughter and son-in-law, Capt. John Nelson, commandant of Mare Island's naval hospital. She and her husband are buried in the Mare Island Cemetery.

The Mare Island Lighthouse is gone, but Vallejo activist Kay Flavell has been working to have a memorial light tower located near the lighthouse site. She envisions the memorial as part of a cultural tourism trail that could include the John Muir home in Martinez, the old State Capitol in Benicia, the Starr mansion in South Vallejo, and other sites.

The 1917 shut-down of the Mare Island Lighthouse was no surprise. After multiple requests by the U.S. Lighthouse Board over several years, Congress had finally voted in 1907 to approve $50,000 for a station on the Vallejo side of the channel. That structure, built on pilings driven into the river bottom 300 yards off Sandy Beach, went into service in 1910. Like the Mare Island station, the new Carquinez Strait Lighthouse also had a long-term head keeper: Charles Kaneen had the post for 25 years.

The Carquinez Strait Lighthouse, which could house a head keeper and two assistants plus their families, remained in service until its 1951 closure by the Coast Guard. Then it was sold to Robert Hubert of San Francisco, operator of a junk-collecting business, who made national news by managing to get it loaded onto a barge and moved under the Carquinez Bridge and up the Carquinez Strait to nearby Elliott Cove.

The Aug. 6, 1955, task was nothing short of Herculean, Vallejo Naval and Historical Museum Executive Director Jim Kern wrote in his 2004 book, *Vallejo*. The 150-ton mansion first had to be detached from the pilings on which it had stood for decades. The next step by a 13-man crew, using house jacks and rollers, was to carefully winch the building onto a 40-by-130-foot barge. Then it was taken in tow by a 600-horsepower tug for a voyage that was short but scary—a passing freighter caused a big wake that made the top-heavy barge rock dangerously.

If Hubert was nervous about the move, he didn't show it. "Nothing can go wrong," he told *Vallejo Times-Herald* reporter Bud Kressin just before the tricky transfer to the barge. "It's just as easy to roll a house onto a barge as it is to roll one along the ground."

Hubert paid only $2 for the lighthouse, but there were conditions: he had to demolish or move the structure. According to wire service stories about the project, most house-movers contacted by Hubert considered him "a trifle crazy"—except for Vallejo house-mover Archie Hanna "who knew the plans weren't insane at all." The lighthouse relocation cost Hubert between $5,000 and $7,000, but the wire service accounts said he felt "it was worth every cent just to prove his sanity."

The Vallejo-side lighthouse was replaced by a smaller automated beacon and fog signal. Minus its tower which was destroyed in the 1955 move, the old lighthouse now serves as the Glen Cove Marina office and a performance and events center. The marina actually is in Elliott Cove, immediately to the west of Glen Cove.

Boris Karloff's Hard Times in Vallejo (Oct. 14, 2018)

This year marks the 200th anniversary of the publication of Mary Shelley's *Frankenstein*— and the 100th anniversary of a stay in Vallejo by a struggling actor named Boris Karloff, who was a dozen years away from fame as the monster in the iconic horror film *Frankenstein*.

A tribute to the lasting influence of Shelley's novel starts Oct. 25 at the Empress Theater with a film screening of *The Bride of Frankenstein*. That will be followed over several days by musical productions, discussions, a screening of local playwright Trevor Allen's *The Creature*, history presentations and more at the Empress, Vallejo Bookstore and Vallejo Naval and Historical Museum. The "Frankenfest" event ends Oct. 31 with a dance contest and screening of *The Rocky Horror Picture Show* at the Empress.

By way of a "Frankenfest" preview, here's the story of how Karloff, in his early 30s, wound up in Vallejo in 1918 long enough to get his name in the town's annual R.L. Polk

& Co. directory. He was listed as an actor at the Airdome Theatre, located at 427 York St., and living with actress Olive de Wilton in an apartment at 614A Capitol St., at the top of the Capitol Street stairs. Some articles list de Wilton as the first of Karloff's four or five spouses, but the records aren't clear on that.

The road to Vallejo was a long one for Karloff, born William Henry Pratt on Nov. 23, 1887, in Camberwell, South London, England. He was expected to follow his father into a Civil Service career, but wanted to act. In 1909, he left for Canada where he started out as a farm-hand and soon began acting in the first of several stock companies. He changed his name to Boris Karloff, picking the first name out of thin air and the second from his mother's family, and acted in hundreds of performances in Canada and Midwest states in the U.S. He also did all sorts of odd jobs when short on cash, which was more often than not. In 1917, Karloff joined Billie Bennett's touring tent show, *The Virginian*, in Chicago. With Karloff in the title role, the troupe worked its way west to Los Angeles, disbanding at the end of the year. He soon joined other theatrical stock companies, including the Robert Lawrence Players and the Maude Amber Players of Vallejo.

There was no shortage of stage performances in Vallejo in 1918, judging from many reviews of plays that ran in local newspapers. In two midsummer reviews in the Vallejo Morning News, he was credited with "some very excellent work" and "an exceptional bit of acting" at the Airdome Theatre—although his name was misspelled as Kariloff. In another review it was misspelled as Koriloff.

On Oct. 8, 1918, reacting to a deadly influenza epidemic, the Vallejo City Council voted unanimously to shut down theaters, dance halls, libraries, schools, churches and other sites used for "public assembly."

That was followed by an Oct. 18 order from the California Board of Health to shut down all theaters in the state. Karloff was out of an acting job again.

"Being addicted to roughly three meals a day, I went to work for the Sperry Flour Mill, waiting for the flu scare to be over so the theater could reopen," Karloff said, according to author Cynthia Lindsay in her 1995 *Dear Boris* biography. Jim Kern, executive director of the Vallejo Naval and Historical Museum, says the mill was a busy place in 1918, having nearly tripled its work force in order to send tons of flour to Europe as part of a World War I relief effort.

Karloff lost his first day's pay because he broke open some flour sacks while loading them. The work was drudgery, but he said he "staggered along" for about two months, piling sacks of flour into trucks and rail cars. By then the flu epidemic had ended— taking the lives of at least 175 people in Vallejo and on Mare Island, according to Dr. Tom Snyder, a retired Vallejo doctor and naval historian. Karloff's acting troupe had disbanded, and by early 1919 he had left Vallejo to join a vaudeville act in San Jose. From there, he worked briefly as an extra in Hollywood, came to San Francisco for more acting that lasted three months, and then went back to Los Angeles for years of bit parts and more odd jobs.

In a 1937 newspaper interview, Karloff said that after leaving Vallejo he thought he had failed in vaudeville and decided to look for work in films in Hollywood. He got small parts but not enough to make a living, and in 1923 took a 40-cents-an-hour job for a building material company unloading sacks of cement. Offered a truck-driving job, Karloff—who had never driven a vehicle—learned the fundamentals by driving

Boris Karloff.

a friend's car around on a vacant lot. The next day, he climbed into the cab of the company's cement truck which he drove for more than a year.

In 1930 Karloff got a small but good role in stage and film versions of *The Criminal Code*. That established him as a villainous heavy, and the next year Universal cast him as the monster in *Frankenstein*. The film cost $275,000 to produce, brought in $12 million in theater rentals and made Karloff an overnight superstar. He went on to more starring roles in *The Bride of Frankenstein*, *The Mummy*, *Son of Frankenstein*, *Scarface* and many other high-profile films. Discussing the monster in a 1962 newspaper interview, Karloff said, "He was the best friend a man ever had."

Over the years he was asked many times what he considered his best horror film. Author Peter Underwood, in his 1971 book, *Karloff—The Life of Boris Karloff*, said the response was always the same: "Without a doubt, the original Frankenstein."

"In over 160 films Karloff portrayed practically every unpleasant character conceivable and just once, really, in 1937 (in the thriller *Night Key*), he tried in a mild way, to rebel against playing horror roles but the critics and the public would have none of it," Underwood wrote. "Horror, or rather terror as Karloff would have preferred it, brought him success, and, willy-nilly, he had to continue to shock and surprise audiences in picture after picture ever after."

Karloff returned to England in 1959, a half-century after he left home for Canada and, eventually, stardom in the U.S. He died on Feb. 2, 1969, at age 81.

The Vallejo *Evening Chronicle's* banner headline announcing the end of World War I on November 11, 1918, was so big that it nearly filled the top half of the newspaper's front page. (*Vallejo Naval and Historical Museum*)

Armistice Ends World War I (Nov. 11, 2018)

One hundred years ago, on Nov. 11, 1918, World War I ended with Germany signing an armistice with the Allies—and "Vallejo went mad today, mad with joy," according to that day's edition of the *Vallejo Evening Chronicle*.

"At three o'clock this morning the prolonged blowing of the big whistle at the navy yard conveyed the first news of the signing of the armistice," the newspaper reported. "There was no formality regarding the announcement on the yard. Offices and shops were summarily dismissed and there was a wild stampede for the boats, every one anxious to get to this side and assist in spreading the news, the best news that has come to the world in four long years."

"Express wagons, dragging empty oil cans, dish pans, or anything else in the way of a noise-maker, raced up and down the streets. People rushed up to each other and shook hands like long, long friends—even if they were only acquaintances."

The shipyard commandant, Capt. Harry George, "sent a naval band and a big detachment of sailors over to help the town celebrate by leading the biggest impromptu parade ever seen in Vallejo. Scores of machines fell into line behind the brave wearers of the Navy blue and cheer upon cheer greeted the enlisted men as they marched through the city."

Twenty Yeomanettes—women who for the first time were authorized to serve in the Navy—were at the head of the parade, marching up Georgia Street; and on the shipyard thousands of sailors were "figuring just how good are the chances of getting a furlough to go home for Thanksgiving," the *Evening Chronicle* said.

"That eleventh day of November, 1918, the Navy Yard practically closed up at ten in the morning," Arnold S. Lott wrote in *A Long Line of Ships*, his book about Mare Island Naval Shipyard. "As the men left the Yard that day many took their work clothes with them. A thousand failed to show up for work the next day, and many of them never did come back. (As late as 1936 the Yard still held 125 unclaimed World War I pay checks.)"

The war had begun on July 28, 1914, with Austria's declaration of war on Serbia. That followed the assassination of Archduke Franz Ferdinand in Sarajevo a month earlier. In early August, Germany declared war on Russia and France, and Britain declared war on Germany. It was not until April 6, 1917, that the United States finally declared war on Germany.

Mare Island Naval Shipyard and Vallejo were transformed by World War I. In early 1917 there were about 3,000 shipyard workers. By the start of 1918 there were about 5,500, and by late fall the number of workers was approaching 10,000.

"Overnight, empty houses and spare rooms in Vallejo became a thing of the past. Workmen lived in garages and tents; they commuted from surrounding cities by auto, ferryboat, and inter-urban trolley," Lott wrote in *A Long Line of Ships*.

During the war a couple of dozen ships were built, including the USS Ward, a destroyer completed in a record-setting 17 ½ days. Hundreds of other ships underwent repairs; and a submarine base, boat shop, a new electrical school and a dozen warehouses were built. New training schools for sailors and Marines were established, and by mid-1917 there were 8,000 sailors and Marines on the shipyard.

Vallejo saloon-keepers were quick to take advantage of the town's overnight population boom—and so were card sharks and local houses of prostitution. That prompted an all-out effort by Capt. George to demand a clean-up. He was backed up by Secretary of the Navy Josephus Daniels, who knew the problems in Vallejo were no different than those in any other Navy town. His solution, in March 1918, was to impose a five-mile zone around all naval bases in the nation where no liquor could be sold. That coincided with enforcement of Prohibition throughout the nation. In Vallejo, Navy investigators also sought to crack down on gambling joints and brothels.

During World War I, more than 116,000 American soldiers, Marines and sailors died from all causes. Research by the Vallejo Naval and Historical Museum showed that included at least 34 men from Vallejo families. The first hometown casualty was Navy sailor Algen Guttridge, whose death was reported in the Nov. 22, 1917, *Vallejo Evening Chronicle*. His ship sank after colliding with another ship off Gibraltar. One of the last casualties was Army Lt. Val Fleming, a Vallejo native who died in combat in France just before the end of the war. News of his death was reported two weeks after the Armistice.

There also were shipyard deaths. On July 9, 1917, Mare Island and Vallejo were rocked by a huge explosion of 2,000 tons of black powder stored at the Naval Ammunition Depot. The blast killed six people and injured 31 others. Investigators determined it was the work of German saboteurs.

With the end of the war in late 1918, activity on Mare Island slowed but the local economy held up well. The 624-foot USS *California*, the biggest ship ever built at Mare Island, was under construction; and the Pacific Fleet was bigger than it had been before the war. Ship-building and overhaul work continued, even throughout the Depression years. By the end of the 1930s there was a dramatic increase in shipyard activity—along with a growing realization that WWI was not going to be the "war to end all wars" that many had hoped it would be. WWII was looming on the horizon.

Mare Island Got First Word on Pearl Harbor Attack (Nov. 25, 2018)

On Sunday morning, Dec. 7, 1941, powerful antennas on the Mare Island shipyard picked up an urgent radio-telegram meant for U.S. Navy ships operating 3,600 miles away near Hawaii—"AIR RAID ON PEARL HARBOR—THIS IS NO DRILL." That was the first stateside word about the devastating surprise attack by Japanese warplanes.

The strafing and bombing started just before 8 a.m. Hawaii time, or 10:30 a.m. PST on Mare Island under the time zone system used in 1941. The radio message went out immediately from Pearl Harbor, and was relayed to top Navy brass in San Francisco by senior telegrapher Van Dayton, on duty in Mare Island's communications office. Less than an hour later, at 11:20 a.m. PST or 2:20 p.m. EST, President Franklin Roosevelt's press secretary, Stephen Early, on a telephone hookup to Associated Press, United Press and International News Service offices in the nation's capital, made the information public.

A flood of national news about Pearl Harbor followed, starting with bulletins from the three news services. That included an all-caps flash filed at 2:22 p.m. EST by AP editor William Peacock, who repeated Early's disparaging term in common use to describe the Japanese—"WHITE HOUSE SAYS JAPS ATTACK PEARL HARBOR."

To commemorate "the day that changed everything" for Mare Island, Vallejo and the nation, the Mare Island Museum is planning a Dec. 7 exhibit of memorabilia including old radio gear and copies of the radio-telegram sent on orders from Lt. Cmdr. Logan Ramsey, operations officer for the Pacific Fleet Air Wing at Pearl Harbor, after he witnessed one of the first Japanese planes flying in low to drop a bomb. At first he thought it was a U.S. plane being flown by a reckless pilot, but then heard the explosion of a delayed-action bomb. The memorial event, starting at 10:30 a.m., will be held at the Mare Island Brewing Co. Taproom, at the foot of Georgia Street in Vallejo.

Ramsey's first radio message was followed by a second one, in the same all-caps format, that stated, "WE ARE AT WAR WITH JAPAN—THIS IS NO DRILL." Then a third message arrived, ordering Mare Island to immediately initiate a war plan that had been prepared in advance and locked in a safe in a shipyard office. Mare Island historian Dennis Kelly says that caused problems—the staffer who had the safe's combination was vacationing at Lake Tahoe. A few hours later, a California Highway Patrol trooper showed up at the door of the man's Tahoe cabin with orders to return at once to Mare Island and open the safe.

The attack by Japanese planes and submarines at the ill-prepared Pearl Harbor base resulted in more than 3,400 U.S. military casualties, including more than 2,300 killed. Twelve ships sank or were beached, and nine other vessels were damaged. More than 180 U.S. aircraft were destroyed and more than 150 others were damaged.

The following day, in an address to a joint session of Congress, President Roosevelt called Dec. 7, 1941, "a date which will live in infamy." Congress then declared war on Japan, abandoning the nation's isolationism policy and ushering the U.S. into World

War II. Within days, Japan's allies, Germany and Italy, declared war on the United States, and the country began a rapid transition to a wartime economy.

The attack on Pearl Harbor galvanized the nation, resulting in an overnight refocusing of all U.S. military, economic, industrial and scientific activity. Work on Mare Island ratcheted up to a level never seen before or since. The day after the attack, crews started pouring cement for bomb shelters on Mare Island. Soon, the Mare Island-Vallejo area was "bristling with anti-aircraft batteries" and "a herd of barrage balloons was tethered above the island, their purpose being to discourage attack by low-flying planes," author Arnold Lott wrote in *A Long Line of Ships*, his book detailing Mare Island's history.

Civilian shipyard employment soared to about 44,000 during the war, with workers coming from almost every state. Sailors, Marines and Army soldiers arrived by the thousands, and Vallejo's pre-war population of about 30,000 tripled. A third of the wartime population lived in hastily constructed housing projects scattered around the city—projects that were filled as soon as they were built. Some workers slept in cars, on porches, in hallways, bathrooms, abandoned shacks, barns, garages or even on the docks. About 300 buses went out in a radius of 75 miles six times a day to pick up workers who lived outside Vallejo.

Mare Island was a key part of a San Francisco Bay area shipbuilding complex that was the largest in the world. During the war, Mare Island workers built 17 submarines, 31 destroyer escorts, 33 assorted small craft and 301 landing craft, and repaired more than 1,200 damaged vessels—including several ships damaged in the Pearl Harbor attack. One of the vessels repaired at Mare Island was the USS Indianapolis, which left in mid-July 1945 on the most secret mission of the war—delivering components of "Little Boy," the world's first operational atomic bomb. The components were unloaded at the island of Tinian on July 26, 1945. Four days later, the Indianapolis headed to Leyte Gulf in the Philippines, was torpedoed and sank. Of the 1,196 men aboard the big cruiser, about 900 made it into the water. After almost five days of shark attacks, starvation, thirst and exposure, 317 men were rescued.

On Aug. 6, 1945, an American B-29 bomber dropped "Little Boy" over Hiroshima. The explosion immediately killed about 80,000 people. Three days later, a second B-29 dropped another A-bomb on Nagasaki, killing an estimated 40,000 people. Japan's Emperor Hirohito announced his country's unconditional surrender in an Aug. 15 radio address, and formal surrender documents were signed Sept. 2 aboard the USS *Missouri* in Tokyo Bay.

3

2019 Columns

"Old 84" on Mare Island Was Navy's First Prison (Jan. 6, 2019)

Mare Island has many claims to fame, starting with its 1854 establishment as the first permanent Navy base on the West Coast. Not so well known is another first—the 1868 construction of a one-story brick building that marked the start of the Navy's land-based prison system.

The prison shut down 78 years later, in 1946 following World War II, after expanding from a small lock-up to a facility large enough to house about 650 inmates. Other prisons were built later by the Navy, but didn't last as long. Next in length of service was the Navy prison in Portsmouth, N.H., which closed in 1973 after 61 years.

Navy prisons were needed following an 1850 congressional ban on flogging sailors with a "cat o' nine tails." Following the ban, the Navy tried alternative punishments ranging from loss of pay or rank to confinement in ship brigs, in irons and subsisting on bread and water. But there was a clear need for a formal prison system, and that system was pioneered on Mare Island.

The Mare Island prison still stands, just north of the old Marine barracks on Flagship Drive on the west side of the shipyard. Visible from the street is a 1901 brick structure, designated Building No. 84; a large concrete wing built on its south side in 1908; and a small 1902 wing on the north side. Another large addition, built in 1938, is at the rear of "Old 84," as it was known throughout the Navy.

A contract for the first prison was awarded in early August 1868, and the work was described as "about completed" in a Dec. 12, 1868, *Vallejo Evening Chronicle* article. A second-story addition was built in the early 1890s, followed by the 1901 brick addition and later expansions.

After closure of Mare Island Naval Shipyard in 1996, Lennar Mare Island became the island's main developer. Lennar had discussed plans to demolish the entire prison due to PCB contamination, but that could change now. The Nimitz Group, a new developer that has shown a deep interest in Mare Island history, has major plans for the north end of the island, and also may acquire Lennar property in the center of the island. That would include the "Old 84" site.

Options other than total demolition include removal of newer additions and restoration of the 1901 brick addition, with its Greek Revival architectural features. At

"Old 84" on Mare Island, dating to 1868, was the navy's first land-based prison. The prison closed in 1946 but the building still stands, minus the tower seen in this 1902 Mare Island Museum shot.

the rear of the 1901 structure, what's left of the original prison, as expanded in 1892, also could be preserved. A 2016 Lennar consultant's report says the 1868 prison was "almost certainly" demolished in 1892, but that doesn't match up with two high-level Navy reports and several Vallejo and San Francisco newspaper stories in the 1890s that I found in researching "Old 84." All those reports and stories describe expansion of the 1868 building. There is no mention of its destruction.

Advocates of partial restoration include retired Navy Capt. Rodney Watterson, author of *Whips to Walls*, a 2014 book that describes the Navy's efforts to revamp its discipline system following the 1850 ban on flogging. Watterson says total demolition of "Old 84" would result in "the permanent loss of an important relic of naval history."

"Old 84" had a reputation as one of the toughest federal prisons. Sailors and Marines who served time there included convicted deserters, mutineers, men who plotted to rob and kill superior officers—and others who just made stupid mistakes.

A series of 1912 stories in the Los Angeles Herald and *San Francisco Call* told of the adventures of a Navy deserter, Jack R. Mosby, who wound up in the Mare Island prison after serving as a general in a Mexican rebel army. Mosby claimed to have served under different flags in Africa, Cuba, South America, the Philippines and China. He said he deserted because of the boredom of U.S. Navy service "in times of peace. It got on my nerves."

USS *California* sailor George Boyog began a 15-year prison term on Mare Island in 1935 following a bold attempt to steal the ship's payroll while at sea. The so-called "battleship bandit" had planned for months to force the disbursing officer to open the ship's safe, take thousands of dollars in cash, and then kill the officer and throw his body overboard. But the officer fought back and Boyog, armed with a revolver, knife and bayonet, was overpowered.

An 1897 news story told of a USS *Philadelphia* sailor named Patrick Mullen who was sentenced to 12 to 18 months in the prison after losing his temper when a Marine stepped on a deck he had just painted. Mullen swore at the Marine, doused him with a bucket of water, and then went ashore without leave, staying drunk for two days.

A search of old newspaper files turned up many accounts of escape attempts, including a Nov. 23, 1893, *San Francisco Call* report about three inmates who cut through bars in the prison tower, where they had been doing some clean-up work. They used hammock ropes to lower themselves about 40 feet to the ground, swam to Vallejo, hopped a freight train to San Francisco and stowed away on a steamer bound for Canada.

In 1920, six prison inmates seized rifles and ammunition and escaped after overpowering and kidnapping Marine guards. A Sept. 6, 1920, *Sacramento Union* account stated that the escapees were recaptured 20 miles away in Cordelia after a gunfight with 25 Marines who were pursuing them. Two of the Marines were wounded.

Stories about escape attempts continued up to World War II. In mid-1943, a sailor on an outside work crew fled after seizing a guard's submachine gun. He was caught nearly two months later working on a ranch in Nevada. The same man escaped again the following December, fleeing with another inmate in a stolen Navy ambulance. They were caught a week later in Utah.

A 1945 Mare Island Grapevine story told how two prisoners working in a wood yard outside the prison changed into civilian clothes they found in a wash room and then headed for Sears Point Road. Authorities caught up with them before they got off the island.

The prison news wasn't only about inmates. A Sept. 10, 1911, story in the *Sacramento Union* recounted the bizarre tale of Capt. Arthur Matthews, the Marine warden of the prison, who committed suicide in Florida several months after embezzling about $3,100 in prison funds. While on the run, the warden, son of a Navy rear admiral, wrote to his brother telling how he crossed into Mexico and joined up with Mexican revolutionaries before deciding to go to Florida.

Filipinos Part of Vallejo-Mare Island "Melting Pot" (Jan. 20, 2019)

The strong ties between the Filipino community and Mare Island Naval Shipyard, dating to the brief Spanish-America War in 1898 and the Philippine-American War that lasted from 1899 to 1903, will be commemorated in a new exhibit to be unveiled Feb. 2 at the Mare Island Museum.

Those ties between Filipinos and the shipyard were not formed overnight. Filipino leaders who helped the U.S. to defeat Spain wanted full independence and resented U.S. acquisition of their country for $20 million. That led to the Philippine-American War, in which more than 4,000 American soldiers and about 20,000 Filipino fighters died. Estimates of Filipino civilians who were killed or died due to disease or hunger during the war ranged from 250,000 to 1 million.

The Vallejo chapter of the Filipino American National Historical Society and the Mare Island Historic Park Foundation collaborated on the upcoming Feb. 2 exhibit, which shows how the 1898 war with Spain and its bloody but little-remembered sequel left Filipinos without the independence they had sought. But they had American "national" status that enabled them to immigrate to America without visas.

Many Filipinos who immigrated here in the early 1900s didn't have to struggle with a language barrier. They had taken English classes at public schools in their homeland, courses that were part of a U.S. effort to create a showcase of American-style democracy in Asia. The Philippines, finally granted independence in 1946, became one of the most Americanized societies in Asia.

Some Filipinos arriving in California were government-sponsored scholars. Others found jobs in canneries or on farms in the Central Valley, or hired out for domestic work in San Francisco. And some were drawn to Vallejo and the prospect of working on Mare Island in jobs that offered good pay, regular shifts and benefits, according to Mel Orpilla, president of the Vallejo chapter of the Filipino American National Historical Society.

Filipinos also were able to join the Navy, although at first their only option was to enlist as stewards and mess attendants. That changed in 1919 at Mare Island with the commissioning of the destroyer USS *Jose Rizal*, named after a Filipino patriot executed by Spain in 1896. The destroyer was manned by about 100 Filipino enlisted sailors, trained at Mare Island to handle all shipboard work under direction of non-Filipino officers. That was a first in U.S. Navy history. The *Jose Rizal* operated throughout the Pacific until it was decommissioned at Mare Island in 1931 and scrapped.

Despite their rapid assimilation into American culture, many discriminatory barriers remained for Filipinos. During the Great Depression, in 1934, Congress limited Filipino

A famous World War II propaganda poster, depicting a wounded Filipino soldier about to toss a grenade, helped to keep up the spirits of Filipino soldiers and civilians during the war. (*Vallejo Naval and Historical Museum*)

immigrants, perceived as a social problem and economic threat, to just 50 people a year. Other laws sought to prevent Filipinos from marrying whites, although Orpilla, in his 2005 *Filipinos in Vallejo* book, says interracial marriages were common here. His book also includes a photo of a Filipino Brownie troop formed because the little girls couldn't join a "white" Brownie troop.

Many Filipinos who tried to get jobs in defense plants at the start of World War II were denied employment at first. But that changed in mid-1941when President Franklin D. Roosevelt issued his famous Executive Order 8802, banning discrimination in defense industry hiring based on race, creed, color or national origin. By 1942, there were about 1,500 Filipinos employed at Mare Island Naval Shipyard.

With the start of World War II, Filipinos from Vallejo enlisted in the military in large numbers. Some who joined the Army were assigned to Filipino infantry battalions and sent to the Philippines to pave the way for Gen. Douglas McArthur's return there. Most of those who enlisted in the Navy didn't get the opportunity that Filipino sailors assigned to the USS *Jose Rizal* had until 1931. Instead of being trained for a wide range of jobs, they were relegated to steward assignments.

At the end of the war, Congress approved the 1946 Rescission Act that denied benefits to Filipinos who served in the Philippine Commonwealth Army under the U.S. military. But Congress also passed the War Brides Act, which gave Filipinos who served in the U.S. military the opportunity to go back to the Philippines, bring home brides and raise "baby boomer" children. Over the years, Vallejo's Asian population has grown to about 30,000, or about a fourth of all the city's residents. Filipinos are the largest segment of that Asian population, totaling about 25,000.

"Families, businesses, community organizations and churches began to build the foundation of the Filipino community as we know it today," Orpilla says. "These Baby Boomers would grow up to become the first ones in their families to graduate from college, become professionals and even follow their parents' footsteps by enlisting in the U.S. military or getting a job at Mare Island."

"The relationship between Mare Island and the Philippines dates back to 1898 and directly led to the employment of thousands of Filipinos until its closing in 1996," Orpilla says. "Filipinos who worked at Mare Island contributed to the operations on Mare Island and subsequently helped shape the Filipino community in Vallejo. It is a rich history that we are proud to share."

Green Book Helped Travelers Avoid Racism (March 17, 2019)

Green Book, the Oscar-winning movie dealing with racism in America in the early 1960s, gets its title from a guidebook that helped African-American travelers find safe places to stop while on the road. The film is set in the Deep South but the travel advice covered areas far beyond that—including Vallejo.

The Negro Motorist Green Book, later renamed *The Negro Travelers' Green Book*, was first published in 1936 by Victor Hugo Green. New editions were released annually until the mid-1960s. The introduction in a 1949 copy said the book's purpose was to help a black traveler "from running into difficulties, embarrassments and to make his trip more enjoyable."

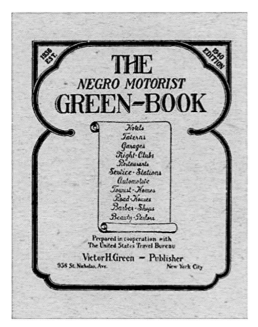

From the 1930s to the 1960s, African-American travelers could rely on *The Negro Motorist Green Book* to help them find restaurants, hotels and other U.S. locations where they would be welcome. (*Vallejo Naval and Historical Museum*)

Thanks to the information on many cities around the country, for restaurants, hotels, motels, service stations and other locations that welcomed everyone, the Green Book was useful. But while Vallejo was included, there were only a few entries over the years, including some that were outdated. Also, some open-door locations known to locals were missing from the book.

The "Green Book" movie is about famed concert pianist Don Shirley and the race-based obstacles and dangers he faced on a concert tour in the Jim Crow South in 1962. His driver, a tough Italian-American bouncer from New York, is forced to rely on Victor Green's guidebook to safely complete the tour. If their trip would have taken them to Vallejo, the only entries in 1962 were for the Bell Motel at 1308 Lincoln Highway and the Charlotte Hotel at 518 Sacramento St.—that had closed a year earlier and was scheduled for demolition. The Bell Motel still exists, now known as Scottish Inns.

If someone had relied on the book in the 1940s or 1950s, the lone Vallejo listing was for a tavern called the Cotton Club, at Virginia and Branciforte streets. The location also had been known as the Corner Club. Not listed were the Knotty Pine, a block away at the corner of Capitol and Branciforte streets, and the 126 Club, a block away in the other direction in the Lower Georgia Street sailor district. Both were well-known gathering spots for African-Americans.

Vallejo's inclusion in the book is no surprise for author Sharon McGriff-Payne, who has chronicled the history of African-Americans in Vallejo area from 1850 on. Her father's Navy duty brought her family here during World War II, the height of the Great Migration that brought many blacks to Vallejo and to readily available jobs at Mare Island Naval Shipyard.

"It was better here but there was still discrimination," McGriff-Payne says. "There were places that just did not cater to African-Americans. It wasn't as bad as the Deep South, but they were not welcome." She also recalls watching her father and two of her uncles map out what they hoped would be a safe route to a family funeral in Florida in the early 1960s. "They were figuring out a way to get through Mississippi and Alabama without stopping, or even going around those states," she says. "Those were states that sent chills up black peoples' spines."

Reaction to the *Green Book* movie has definitely been mixed. While it's a big box-office success, the film has been harshly criticized by Don Shirley's family as a misrepresentation of facts—including the idea that the pianist and his driver, Tony "Lip" Vallelonga, became life-long friends as a result of their road trip. Shirley's brother, Maurice Shirley, also dismissed as bogus the depiction of Shirley as isolated from his family and alienated from his own black culture. And some film critics say the film, however well-intentioned, oversimplifies a major issue by suggesting that racism is a problem that can be easily solved.

The movie does succeed in showing the need for Victor Hugo Green's guidebook, during a period of racial problems so severe that many African-Americans relied on it to know which businesses they should patronize while traveling across America. The first Green Book started with only 10 pages, and grew with each year's edition to eventually include pictures, stories, advertisements and a vacation guide. The 1966–1967 Green Book was the last edition to be published, two years after the 1964 Civil Rights Act brought an end to legal segregation.

"You always know that with movies things will be changed to suit the plot. But the book did help people to know how to travel and where to travel," McGriff-Payne says. "The fact that there was a Green Book is an important reminder that racism existed and got in the way of people being able to live normal lives. Travel is supposed to be wonderful—but instead you had to travel in fear."

Who Was Admiral Callaghan? (March 31, 2019)

Vallejo and Mare Island have many streets named in honor of former Mare Island Naval Shipyard commandants and other top Navy officers. The list includes Alden, Baldwin, Craven, Cunningham, Farragut, Gardner, Mayo, McDougal, Parrott, Rodgers, Selfridge, Tisdale and others. Only one of these streets—the busiest of all—clearly makes the Navy connection by including the officer's rank: Admiral Callaghan Lane.

This 3-mile-long lane, running through major Vallejo shopping zones along the east side of Interstate 80 between Tennessee Street and Columbus Parkway, is named for Rear Adm. Daniel Judson Callaghan Sr. The Navy hero, a San Francisco native, died when his flagship, the USS *San Francisco*, was shelled repeatedly during a major World War II sea battle against Japanese warships. More than 100 of the ship's crew died in what became variously known as the Naval Battle of Guadalcanal, the Battle of Savo Island or the Battle of Friday the 13th.

Callaghan, awarded the Congressional Medal of Honor after his death, had many connections to Mare Island Naval Shipyard and to Vallejo over the years, starting in 1911 when he reported for duty aboard his first ship, the USS *California*, which was

Admiral Callaghan Lane, one of Vallejo's busiest streets, is named in honor of Navy Adm. Daniel Judson Callaghan, who died aboard his flagship, USS *San Francisco*, in a major WWII naval battle. (*Vallejo Naval and Historical Museum*)

at the shipyard. The Navy cruiser, that predated the Mare Island-built battleship by the same name, was in and out of San Francisco Bay on a regular basis.

On one of the cruiser's in-port stops, Callaghan ran into a childhood friend, Mary Tormey of Oakland, a distant cousin of Vallejo Mayor William J. Tormey. Dan and Mary began dating, and in 1914, after he had been reassigned to the destroyer USS *Truxtun*, at Mare Island for a full overhaul, they were married.

In the 1930s, on San Francisco-based shore duty, Callaghan was at Mare Island many times, conducting ship inspections. In 1938, with the rank of commander and about to be promoted to captain, he signed on as President Franklin Roosevelt's naval aide and accompanied Roosevelt to Mare Island in July that year.

After nearly three years ashore as the president's naval aide, Callaghan requested sea duty and was given command of the Mare Island-built USS *San Francisco* on March 17, 1941. He spent most of April at the Mare Island Naval Hospital, suffering from a digestive attack, and finally boarded his ship on May 27 in Honolulu. The ship was in Pearl Harbor during the Dec. 7, 1941, surprise attack by Japanese forces, but wasn't damaged. A few weeks later, the cruiser headed out to sea for 2½ months of combat duty.

In April 1942, the San Francisco was ordered to return to Mare Island for repairs. It was Callaghan's last stop at the shipyard. While the repairs were being made, he was temporarily reassigned to a high-level command working on battle plans in the South Pacific. In a period of a few months, he was promoted to rear admiral and ordered to take over a new combat task force of destroyers and cruisers, including the San Francisco which had returned to the war zone. He rejoined the ship in late October.

A few weeks later, on Friday, Nov. 13, Callaghan's task force steamed into the middle of a large Japanese Navy fleet with three times its firepower. The Japanese ships were a key part of plan to wipe out U.S. troops on the strategically located island of Guadalcanal with its important airstrip, Henderson Field. When told that an attack on the enemy ships would be suicide, Callaghan replied, "Yes, I know, but we have to do it." A few minutes after his order to "get the big ones [Japanese battleships] first," Callaghan was killed when the bridge of his ship took a direct hit.

The chaotic battle, fought in the dark at point-blank range, lasted only about half an hour. When it was over, the Americans had lost two cruisers and four destroyers. The San Francisco, badly damaged but afloat, was credited with crippling a Japanese battleship that became an easy target for U.S. bombers the next day and was scuttled. Callaghan's ship also was credited with sinking or damaging other enemy ships. The remaining Japanese fleet had fled, and Henderson Field had been saved from a major assault. Naval historian Paul Dull has described the sea battle as "the most confused, close-ranged, and horrendous surface engagement of the war."

Callaghan was buried at sea and the San Francisco returned to Mare Island for repairs. The ship then went back to the Pacific Theater and was involved in extensive combat duty. Its damaged bridge was stored at Mare Island until 1950 and was then made part of a permanent memorial at Land's End in San Francisco. At the end of the war, the San Francisco returned to Mare Island for a few weeks and then made a final voyage in January 1946 to Philadelphia where it was placed in reserve. The ship was sold for scrap in 1959.

In mid-October 1951, Callaghan's son, Daniel J. Callaghan Jr., came to Vallejo for the dedication of Admiral Callaghan Lane. Callaghan Jr., a WWII Navy veteran and state director of veterans affairs, said the event was "not only for my father but for the entire Navy and for every man who gave his life during the war." He was joined by many military and civic leaders, including retired Vice Adm. M. S. Tisdale, a classmate and life-long friend of Adm. Callaghan. Members of American Legion Post 550, which fronts on the lane, had asked for the name change, noting Callaghan's ties to Mare Island and his status as a distinguished U.S. Navy hero.

While a street sign with the new name was erected as part of the ceremony, city directories continued to list the old name, Lincoln Highway, for the addresses of the Post 550 building and other properties along the road. The old addresses were finally dropped following formal approvals of the new name in 1958 by both the Vallejo City Council and Solano County supervisors.

Vallejo's Alley History (April 14, 2019)

A century ago, city officials chose names of cars, in alphabetical order, for 23 Vallejo alleys. There have been many articles about the names over the years, but writers ran into some dead ends in explaining the details. Here's another attempt to get the facts straight—especially about Indian Alley, between Georgia and Virginia streets.

The alley names came from Tobias "Tobe" Kilkenny, city engineer and superintendent of streets, in 1916. In a 1952 interview, he told *Times-Herald* reporter Herb Levy that he was directed to identify the alleys and "so I sat down and gave them names.

If you want to explore Vallejo alleys named after cars, the 400 block of Indian Alley has interesting architecture and a mural that mimics the style of famed painter Vincent Van Gogh. (*Vallejo Naval and Historical Museum*)

I gave them names that were familiar to the people of Vallejo, which happened to be names of automobiles." That seems clear enough—he had cars in mind when he picked the Indian Alley name. But years later, after Kilkenny had passed away, difficulty in finding information on Indian cars apparently led to the idea that he was thinking of well-known Indian motorcycles. However, records in the National Automobile Museum in Reno show there were Indian cars, mostly experimental, produced by the Hendee Manufacturing Co. in Springfield, Mass. But George Hendee wanted to steer his company away from cars and focus on motorcycles. By the 1920s the firm had become the Indian Motorcycle Co.

Jackie Frady, the museum's executive director, cites the Standard Catalog of American Cars, 1805–1942—the exhaustive, 1,612-page bible for anyone looking into the history of U.S.-made vehicles. The catalog of more than 5,000 car companies, first published in 1985, shows that Hendee's first four-wheelers were built shortly after the company was founded in 1905 and the last—including three that still exist—were produced in the late 1920s.

Other confusing aspects include the fact that today, despite the alphabetical layout, you can't find an alley starting with the letters A, B or C. The city's alley signs start with Dodge, a one-block lane between Curtola Parkway and Jersey Street. But the original designations in 1916 started with Abbott, followed by Buick and Cadillac alleys. When Kilkenny came up with his list of names, the city was in the middle of a major dredge-and-fill project that eventually turned a large tidal area south of Curtola Parkway (formerly Maryland Street) into usable land. He was getting street and alley names in place ahead of time, while the watery area was being filled with Napa River mud. Due to industrial development in recent years, the A, B and C alleys disappeared.

Most of the named alleys run in an east-west direction, parallel to city streets that are named after states. But there are a couple of north-south exceptions, Winton and Young alleys, short stretches, mostly dirt, between Amador and Contra Costa streets next to Children's Wonderland. Rambler Alley, another short, north-south lane, was added to the city's list after the 1916 alley designations. It runs along the east side of Interstate 80 between Georgia Street and Benicia Road. The original R alley is Reo, between Tennessee and Indiana streets. Other alleys, not named, are near Rambler Alley, including one that starts at Jennings Avenue, crosses Laurel Street and ends at Russell Street.

Due to overgrown vegetation, it's almost impossible to spot unmarked Holly Alley, which on old maps runs between C and D streets in Bay Terrace, near the Mira Theatre. Longtime Bay Terrace residents say the alley, another addition that followed the 1916 list, may have once been wide enough for cars but for decades has only been a footpath. And it's not the only such alley in that neighborhood—there are a few more that don't have names.

Other no-name alleys around town include two just north of Vallejo High School, on either side of Nevada Street. Also, a block east of Tuolumne Street, an alley runs between Valle Vista and Greenfield avenues.

There's no chance of using the original 1916 list to find Thomas Alley, between Arkansas and Illinois streets. In 1931 it was changed to Templar Alley to clear up any confusion with Thomas Avenue, which runs between Benicia Road and Curtola Parkway.

Here's a current list, in case you want to take a walking or driving tour of our alleys with car names, starting on the south side of town and heading north: Dodge, Everett, Ford, Garford, Hudson, Indian, Jeffrey, Kissell, Lozier, Maxwell, National, Overland, Packard, Quincy, Rambler, Reo, Stutz and Templar. Then head over to the south side of Children's Wonderland to find what's left of unmarked Winton and Young alleys. Velie Alley runs for one block between Sacramento Street and Yolo Avenue, just south of Nebraska Street.

There's a Pollack Alley that runs off Azuar Avenue on Mare Island, near Touro University California. The alley gets its name from a submarine, the USS *Pollack*—that was named after a fish resembling a cod, not a car. Also, vehicles can get through some narrow-paved strips between industrial buildings on Mare Island, although those lanes aren't marked as alleys.

No doubt there are other alleys not listed here. If you know about them, let me know. This is a topic that's always good for an update—maybe a wide-ranging account of what went on in the alleys. There was plenty of illicit activity in Hudson and Indian alleys, on either side of Lower Georgia Street with its many bars, bordellos and gambling houses that flourished during World War II. Other stories involve dads working on the family car, and kids riding bikes and coasters down steep alleys or tossing basketballs into hoops mounted on garages—the expected fabric of just about any neighborhood. Then there's the unexpected—like a 1935 FBI report about gangster George "Baby Face" Nelson counting out stacks of money in his car parked in Quincy Alley, behind the old Vallejo General Hospital run by his friend Tobe Williams. But all those tales will have to be column material for another day.

Vallejo's Alibi Clock Needs an Alibi (May 12, 2019)

Labor radical Tom Mooney thought he had an alibi to refute charges he planted a bomb that killed 10 people and wounded 40 others in 1916: A photo showed him watching a much-publicized parade more than a mile away when the bomb exploded near the

Vallejo's Alibi Clock, at 316 Georgia St., is said to have figured in drawn-out defense efforts to free labor radical Tom Mooney, imprisoned for 22½ years for a 1916 bombing that killed ten people and wounded forty others in San Francisco. (*Vallejo Naval and Historical Museum*)

San Francisco waterfront. A sidewalk clock in that photo confirmed the exact time. For decades a 20-foot-tall timepiece, moved from the city to Vallejo in 1932, has been known as the same clock—but now needs its own alibi.

Here's the problem: An extensive San Francisco photo collection assembled by author Jack Tillmany includes a March 1917 image showing a ball-shaped sidewalk clock at the same 928 Market St. location as the clock in Mooney's famous July 22, 1916, photo. It's clearly different than Vallejo's square-shaped Alibi Clock, which doesn't appear in other photos of that 900 block of Market Street until after the bombing, on the sidewalk a few doors down at 938 Market St.

I'm posting several photos on Facebook and hoping that someone out there can find more that will produce the alibi that Vallejo's Alibi Clock needs: a mid-1916 shot with better detail of the clock in Mooney's photo. That July 1916 image clearly shows him, but the background is fuzzy. You can't tell the clock's shape and can barely make out the 2:01 p.m. time, five minutes before the bomb exploded. If a better 1916 shot shows it was square-shaped, you could assume it was replaced not long after the bombing by the ball-shaped clock seen in the August 1917 photo, and then reinstalled a few years later at 938 Market St.—thereby qualifying it as our Alibi Clock. Seems like a stretch, but here's hoping that this mystery can be solved and the Vallejo clock proves to be authentic.

Mooney figured that his 1916 photo would help him avoid a long prison term for the bombing near the city's Embarcadero, but it didn't work out that way. Instead, Mooney finally was pardoned in 1939, after spending 22½ years behind bars due to a corrupt prosecutor's lies, popular prejudice and the repeated failure of authorities to acknowledge the obvious: he wasn't anywhere near the explosion.

The bombing was portrayed as an act of anarchists opposed to American military involvement in World War I. The blast occurred at the starting point of a parade that was one of many "Preparedness Day" events held around the country to drum up support for that military involvement. Mooney and another labor radical, Warren Billings, were convicted in a case that became an international cause celebre for radicals, trade unionists and defenders of civil liberties who insisted both men were framed. Billings also spent more than 20 years in prison until finally winning a commutation to time served.

Those supporting Mooney and Billings in their long struggle for freedom included crusading newspaper editor Fremont Older, who at first believed Mooney was guilty but then learned a key prosecution witness, Frank Oxman, lied on the stand—at the urging of the city's district attorney, Charles Fickert. Oxman testified that he saw Billings and Mooney in a car, with Mooney carrying a suitcase, headed toward the spot where the suitcase bomb was planted. But Older learned of letters Oxman wrote indicating he wasn't even in San Francisco at the time, and published those letters on the front page of the *San Francisco Evening Bulletin*.

Older and others "conducted further investigation that demonstrated that the prosecution's cases against Billings and Mooney were completely fraudulent: prosecution witnesses contradicted themselves and one another; they were paid to testify; the jury foreman in Mooney's trial was in collusion with the district attorney's office. Support for the defendants spread nationally and internationally," author John C. Ralston wrote in his 2013 book, *Fremont Older and the 1916 San Francisco Bombing: A Tireless Crusade for Justice*.

San Francisco city directories list H. Cohn & Co. Jewelers at 928 Market St., where the ball-shaped clock was located, in 1916. In 1924 a Burnett Bros. jewelry store opened at 938 Market St., and the square-shaped clock was definitely located there until that store closed in 1932. The four-faced clock, manufactured in 1907, was then hauled to the Burnett Bros. shop at 320 Georgia St. in Vallejo. That same year, Richard Simon, who had been secretary-treasurer of the Burnett Bros. store chain in California, filed a claim stating the chain was deeply in the red and owed him $13,000. A few months later, he took over as owner of the Vallejo store and changed its name to the Simon Company. In his newspaper ads, the shop was termed "The Home of the Big Clock."

Simon's had a long run in Vallejo, finally closing in 1984. The city then bought the clock, designated it as a Vallejo landmark and moved it to a nearby sidewalk location in front of Brown's Jewelers, at 316 Georgia St. The Brown family took care of the clock until store owner Robert Brown Sr. died in 2009 and the business closed. After that, the city took over maintenance of the clock's iron case. City workers also wind the clock twice a week. Work on the gears and other internal parts of the old clock's movement is handled by Dorian Clair, a San Francisco clock repair expert.

Will our Alibi Clock turn out to be the real deal, an important reminder of the dangers of overreaction and injustice during national crises? Or will its claimed status turn out to be a mistake or, worse, a made-up tale to enhance its advertising value for a jewelry store? And no matter what further research reveals about its authenticity, will the clock keep running and remain a downtown Vallejo landmark despite being exposed to the elements and targeted from time to time by vandals? Recycling a tired cliché seems appropriate in this case: Only time will tell.

Vallejo's Greatest WWII Hero—Army Air Ace Grant Mahony (May 26, 2019)

Memorial Day is a day to remember the men and women, including many with Vallejo ties, who died in the defense of our country. This column is about one of them—Army Air Corps ace Grattan "Grant" Mahony, a Vallejo boy who became a national hero, flying more combat missions and hours than any other U.S. aviator in World War II before being shot down as the war neared an end.

Mahony flew at least 550 combat missions, with close to 1,000 combat hours, in the Philippines, Java, Australia, China and Burma. On Jan. 3, 1945, returning from a U.S. attack on an enemy airfield in the Philippines, he spotted a moored Japanese seaplane and decided to strafe it. But the plane was a decoy, with many anti-aircraft guns hidden on the nearby shore. His P-30 Lightning plane was hit in the wing, caught fire and crashed into the jungle. A month went by before his family learned he had died.

A 26-year-old lieutenant colonel at the time of his death, Mahony was one of the most decorated American fighter pilots in WWII. He was credited with downing five Japanese planes, and possibly several others, in air-to-air combat and destroying at least two dozen more that were on enemy runways or at float plane bases. In strafing and bombing runs, he also destroyed or damaged many locomotives, buildings including a military radio station, and heavy equipment including a steamroller. In one dare-devil flight in 1941, he flew low over Japanese ground troops while two pursuing enemy planes were firing at him and realized his maneuver caused those planes strafe their own troops—so he looped around and flew the same course, and the pilots strafed their own troops again. Then he managed to

Grattan "Grant" Mahony grew up in Vallejo and in World War II became a national hero, flying more combat missions than any other U.S. aviator during the war. (*Vallejo Naval and Historical Museum*)

get away with no major hits to his plane. A member of the Flying Tigers, he was named the "most chased" pilot in the Far East in a 1942 war dispatch. His many awards included the Distinguished Service Cross, 11 Air Medals, four presidential citations, three Distinguished Flying Crosses, two Silver Stars, a dozen battle service stars, Purple Heart and other honors.

Mahony was sent back to the states for a few months in 1943 prior to heading back to the Pacific war zone for his third and final combat duty tour. While in Vallejo in July 1943, he was honored at a massive welcome-home event attended by tens of thousands of people, according to various newspaper accounts. It was described as the biggest civic celebration in Vallejo history.

Mahony "comes home today not only a 'home town' hero, but a national hero—one of many, but one whose heroism has spread to the four corners of the United States," the *Vallejo Times-Herald* declared.

At the conclusion of a long parade through town, the unassuming war hero said, "I wasn't selected to be up here because my name's Mahony. I am here only because I am in the uniform of the thousands of men and women from Vallejo who are serving their nation. This is their affair." Then he described some of his wartime experiences, including his reason for targeting a Japanese military radio station while flying with other U.S. planes in the Philippines. He said another pilot, Bob Hanson from Oakland, began singing his school song over an intercom and the radio station operator, apparently thinking Hanson was using some type of code, jammed the wave length. "So I started to sing, 'Hail, Vallejo Junior High.' Then they really jammed the wave length," Mahony said. "So we shot up their radio station so we could go on singing."

Longtime Vallejo journalist Marion Devlin, recounting her memory of the big 1943 event that honored Mahony, said in a 1984 Vallejo Independent Press column that he deserved all the attention "but his luck ran out, and Grant Mahony, like so many other young Vallejoans, lost his life in the final stages of the war." Devlin said she stopped by the memorial rose garden in Grant Mahony Park, at the corner of Illinois and Mariposa streets just off Tennessee Street, adding, "It is well worth a visit, not only to enjoy the roses but to stir again memories of Grant Mahony, and of a war that claimed so many fine young lives."

Those memories of Grant Mahony still exist for some, especially longtime Vallejoans. But for many others he's an unknown, aviation historian Jack Cook says. "He's one of those guys who did an amazing amount during the war. He had a belief about having no combat exhaustion. He was always trying to get back overseas," Cook adds. "But even among people interested in wartime aviation, I would say only one out of 1,000 knows about him. It's a shame that he's largely forgotten."

Besides the city park named for the heroic aviator, maintained by the Greater Vallejo Recreation District with help from the North Bay Rose Society, the Veterans of Foreign Wars named one of its local posts for Mahony. A military air field in the Philippines also was named for Mahony, whose grave is in the Manila American Cemetery in Taguig City, Philippines.

Mare Island Deeds and Misdeeds (June 9, 2019)

Historical research can take you down a rabbit-hole of conflicting information that gets curiouser and curiouser the more you read. That's what happens when trying to sort out how and why Mare Island changed hands over the years and who wound up with proper deeds.

At first glance, it seems clear enough: The island was granted by the Mexican government to Victor Castro in 1841. In 1853 the U.S. Navy bought the island, and a year later opened a shipyard that operated until 1996. The city of Vallejo then got the island, retained some acreage but turned over the large central core, mainly to housing developer Lennar. A sale of Lennar's interests to the Nimitz Group is now in the works. But that snapshot leaves out a tangled web of early-day fraud, sweetheart deals, and decades-long legal battles that reached the U.S. Supreme Court.

The most detailed accounts of Mare Island's ownership history start with Victor Castro's claim of an 1841 grant from Juan Alvarado, governor of the Mexican province of California and Castro's brother-in-law. Castro needed a safe place to graze his horses because local Indians were stealing them on the mainland. In late 1847, Castro sold the island to William and Lucy Bryant for $800, who several months later sold their interest to Stephen and Melinda Cooper for $441. The Coopers in turn recorded a sale of the island in August 1850 to two sons, two nephews and three other young men—who then left for the California gold fields. The wily Castro, seeing a new opportunity, followed up on the Bryant-Cooper deals by selling the island again—this time for a reported $7,500. The sale to Bezar Simmons and John Frisbie, Gen. Mariano Vallejo's son-in-law, was recorded in December 1851. Castro retained a 1/10th interest.

Frisbie wanted the Navy to choose Mare Island for a West Coast shipyard location. For $469, he and Simmons sold a small interest in the island to Lt. William McArthur, the Navy surveyor assigned to the shipyard search, in an obvious bid for his recommendation. By mid-1852, in deals totaling $13,300, wealthy entrepreneur William Aspinwall and George Bissell had bought out Frisbie, Simmons and Castro. Six months later, on Jan. 4, 1853, the Navy paid $83,491 for the Aspinwall-Bissell-McArthur interests—a 100-fold increase over the Bryants' $800 cost in 1847. The Navy's title was confirmed in 1855 by a government panel set up to adjudicate various land claims in California; and was again confirmed in March 1857 by a federal court decree.

All that wheeling and dealing was complicated enough, but it didn't stop there. In 1877, 23 years after Mare Island Naval Shipyard had opened, the 1847–50 Bryant-Cooper deals formed the basis of a claim by D. W. Bouldin, son of one of the seven men who bought island from the Coopers. That lawsuit took years to resolve, with a federal court finally ruling in March 1887 against Bouldin's ownership claim. Bouldin had many favorable witnesses but couldn't produce adequate records. One official record book was missing and another one had pages torn out. He did produce a grant deed from Gov. Alvarado to Castro, allegedly signed in May 1841. But the court ruled it was fraudulent—apparently signed after Mexico had ceded California to the United States. Efforts to revive the case continued without success until 1895. Why was the original Alvarado grant to Castro rejected in the Bouldin case but not challenged years earlier in the Navy's 1855–7 title confirmation process? Additional research is needed to answer that question.

There's more, including statements by Castro that he had made out two more deeds to lawyers who said they could recover Mare Island for him—providing they got a half interest. Those schemes went nowhere, but questions about ownership of swamp land on the north end and just north of Mare Island led to court actions that began in 1886 and continued until 1942. Two cases, involving thousands of acres of land, reached the

A lithograph drawn by Charles Braddock Gifford depicts Mare Island in about 1860. There were many lawsuits over ownership of the island. (*Vallejo Naval and Historical Museum*)

U.S. Supreme Court. In one case, a lower court ruling favorable to wealthy oilman James O'Donnell resulted in armed Marines doing sentry duty in November 1927 to prevent anyone from homesteading on what the Navy considered its land. The Navy ignored an eviction notice delivered by O'Donnell, barred him from any access to the property, and appealed to the Supreme Court. Finally, in March 1938, the high court reversed the lower court and held that the Navy had valid title to nearly 1,500 acres claimed by O'Donnell. He headed a group of several people who traced their claims to David Darlington, to whom the state of California had conveyed the acreage on the north end of the island in 1857, under terms of the federal Swamp Land Act of 1850.

The Navy lost in another case decided in May 1942 by the nation's highest court. The decision, involving several thousand acres of tideland just north of Mare Island, favored the West End Land Co., Field and Tule Land Co., Bay Land Co., Sears Point Toll Road Co., James Irvine and Mary Stewart. In its ruling on that dispute, the Supreme Court held that the property sought by the Navy wasn't part of the original Mexican land grant to Victor Castro.

Disputes over Mare Island acreage continued even after the closure of the shipyard in 1996. When the Navy began to dispose of the base, the state of California challenged the Navy's view that the Supreme Court's 1938 decision in the O'Donnell case had identified the extent of federally owned lands on the island. The conflict effectively clouded title to the property, and that led to several years of negotiations between the state and the city of Vallejo. Finally, in 2002, a 300-page agreement cleared the way for new development on Mare Island. "We used to have a joke on Mare Island Naval

Shipyard that a ship couldn't leave until the weight of the paperwork generated during the overhaul equaled the weight of the ship," Mare Island Museum historian Dennis Kelly wrote in a 2016 article about the shipyard's property disputes. "Apparently the joke was also applicable to the redevelopment of Mare Island."

City Recognizes African-American Sailors Charged with Mutiny in Vallejo (July 7, 2019)

After 75 years, Vallejo is finally commemorating African-American sailors who died in a massive 1944 munitions explosion at Port Chicago—and honoring other black sailors who survived, were sent to Vallejo and then refused to load more bombs under hazardous conditions that led to the blast. The explosion and the survivors' actions, labeled mutiny by the Navy, triggered efforts to curb pervasive racism in our nation's Armed Services.

The mutiny convictions of the shell-shocked "Port Chicago 50" followed the July 17, 1944, explosions that killed 320 men, 202 of them African-American sailors, and injured 390 others—the worst home-front disaster of World War II.

Memorial events have been held for many years at the site of the Port Chicago ammunition depot. A proclamation prepared by City Council member Katy Miessner for a presentation by Mayor Bob Sampayan appears to be Vallejo's first formal recognition that the disaster and the so-called "mutiny" that followed on Aug. 9, 1944, helped to eventually integrate our military.

Miessner worked with Vallejo historian and author Sharon McGriff-Payne on the proclamation, which was approved at a recent City Council meeting. McGriff-Payne is the daughter of Marshall McGriff, one of the black sailors sent to Mare Island in WWII and assigned to the ammunition dump on the shipyard. He knew many of the sailors who were killed at Port Chicago and others who refused to return to work loading ammunition.

McGriff-Payne says the tragedy had a profound impact on the African-American community in Vallejo and the rest of the San Francisco Bay area. She adds that the Vallejo branch of the National Association for the Advancement of Colored People, with leaders including Frank Shipp and Arthur Scott, played pivotal roles in drawing national attention to the historic events.

Also planned is a memorial at the end of Ryder Street, on the Vallejo side of the Mare Island Strait. After the surviving sailors were sent to Vallejo following the explosion, they were ordered to board a ferry at the old Ryder Street pier and go to Mare Island for more bomb-loading. Their refusal to do so resulted in the largest mutiny trial in U.S. Navy history.

In *The Port Chicago 50: Disaster, Mutiny, and the Fight for Civil Rights*, author Steve Sheinkin says that as the nation raced to prepare for war, civil rights groups challenged the Navy to abolish its racial restrictions. However, Secretary of the Navy Frank Knox insisted there was nothing he could do.

President Roosevelt supported the Navy secretary's decision. But Roosevelt was also a politician. He counted on strong support from African American voters, and was being pressured by black leaders to do something about the military's racial policies. So the president looked for a compromise.

African-American sailors load ammunition at the Port Chicago ammunition depot during World War II. A massive explosion at the depot destroyed two ships and killed 320 men. Surviving black sailors were sent to Vallejo, and many wound up facing mutiny charges for refusing to continue loading bombs. (*Vallejo Naval and Historical Museum*)

In April 1942, Secretary Knox unveiled a policy change to ensure that black volunteers could get better training. But they still could not serve aboard ships at sea except as mess attendants. Dissatisfaction among African-American sailors increased. Race-based conflicts included riots in Vallejo involving hundreds of sailors in late 1942 and early 1943. Nothing brought the Navy's segregationist policies into sharper focus than the rioting in Vallejo and elsewhere, the Port Chicago explosion and the mutiny trial.

The huge Port Chicago blast destroyed two cargo ships, the *Quinault Victory* and the *E.A. Bryan*, wrecked the Navy base and damaged the nearby town of Port Chicago. Other communities in the area, including Vallejo, also sustained damage. Seismograph machines recorded two jolts measuring 3.4 on the Richter scale. The *E.A. Bryan* was blown to bits, and the *Quinault Victory* was lifted out of the water, turned around and broken into pieces. Both ships were about 440 feet in length. The explosive force of the blast was equivalent to five kilotons of TNT, on the same order of magnitude as the atomic bomb that was dropped on Hiroshima just over a year later.

On July 31, 1944, 328 black sailors who survived the explosion were transferred to Vallejo, and they realized there would be no work other than more ammunition loading. Author Robert Allen, in *The Port Chicago Mutiny*, wrote that the men, fearful of another explosion and angry about their treatment, "began talking of not going back to work. For many, the risk of another explosion was uppermost in their minds."

On Aug. 9, they were ordered to march toward a ferry that would take them across the Napa River to the Mare Island ammunition depot, and 258 of the 328 men wound up being confined to a barge after refusing to go. A Navy admiral told the sailors that mutiny in time of war carried a death sentence, but Allen said 50 sailors "refused to be cowed" and in early September were charged with conspiring to mutiny.

On Oct. 24, at the end of a month-long trial and after only eight minutes of deliberation, the military court found all 50 defendants guilty. Each man was sentenced to 15 years in prison. A few weeks later, the sentences were reviewed and 40 were reduced to prison time ranging from eight to 12 years. Despite appeals from NAACP Legal Defense Fund lawyer Thurgood Marshall, later a U.S. Supreme Court justice, First Lady Eleanor Roosevelt and others, the convictions were upheld in mid-1945. But then, with the Japanese surrender following the atomic bombing of Hiroshima and Nagasaki, the sentences were further reduced. Finally, in January 1946, 47 of the men were freed. Two others who had been in a prison hospital were released soon after that. One sailor with a bad-conduct record served additional time and was then released.

Starting in late 1944, under Navy Secretary James Forrestal's guidance, steps toward desegregation were taken. In February 1946, just a month after the Port Chicago prisoners were released, the Navy became the first branch of the U.S. military to officially eliminate all racial barriers. The Navy's decision to end segregation led to an even bigger change: Impressed by the progress being made in the Navy, President Harry Truman on July 26, 1948, issued an executive order to ensure desegregation and equal opportunity in all branches of the service.

Besides McGriff-Payne and Miessner, Liat Meitzenheimer, Brien Farrell and I were in an ad hoc group that initially sought the proclamation. Also involved in the effort were Vallejo Sanitation & Flood Control District, located at the end of Ryder Street, and Kiewit Pacific Co., which provided access at its Vallejo yard to the old Ryder Street pier location.

Vallejo's Carnegie Library Bulldozed During Redevelopment (Sept. 1, 2019)

Any discussion of Vallejo's massive redevelopment project a half-century ago invariably leads to this question: What in the world were officials thinking when they insisted that the list of 500-plus buildings to be bulldozed had to include the city's grand Andrew Carnegie Library?

A review of old newspaper articles shows there were several opportunities throughout the 1960s to change course and preserve the old library, which stood on the northwest corner of Sacramento and Virginia streets. But redevelopment proponents finally got their way, and the library, dedicated on July 4, 1904, and opened on March 2, 1905, was reduced to rubble in 1970.

Congress launched urban renewal on a national level with the Housing Act of 1949, providing federal funding to cover two-thirds of many redevelopment costs. Vallejo followed up in 1956 by creating the Vallejo Redevelopment Agency (VRA), headed by Jim Richardson, for its massive Marina Vista project. As the agency worked on demolition plans, a 1959 study to evaluate the library's needs concluded that it was inadequate to serve the community.

A "Save the Library" move started quickly, with calls for converting it into a historical museum. Several preservation advocates asked the City Council in 1961 to support the idea—but council members took no action, ducking the issue by saying the building already was on the VRA's list of structures to be bulldozed.

In late 1962 the Carnegie Library won a conditional reprieve, with Richardson stating it could be spared if found to be structurally safe and if a financially responsible person or organization would guarantee to rehabilitate and maintain the building. City Building Inspector Clifton Yeomans said the library was structurally sound, but members of the Solano County Historical Society were divided on the idea of taking over the building. Some favored the museum plan while others said the society lacked the funds to operate the building as a museum without financial assistance from the city and Solano County.

In early 1964, Mayor Florence Douglas stirred things up by saying the plan for a new library and city hall in the center of the redevelopment zone should be scrapped, and instead a large auditorium-convention center should be built there. Douglas said that would encourage more commercial activity while the old library and old city hall could be expanded.

Redevelopment advocates countered that a new library and city hall were essential elements of a civic center complex—and the old Carnegie Library was no "architectural gem" deserving of preservation. As Vallejoans prepared to vote on a $2.4 million bond issue to finance the new library, state Sen. Luther Gibson, publisher of the morning *Times-Herald* and evening *News Chronicle*, ran ads stating, "Our old library has to go." He added the bond issue was backed by the Chamber of Commerce, Central Labor Council, Downtown Association and other groups.

But when the ballots cast in the Nov. 3, 1964, election were counted, the proponents of the new library had narrowly failed to get the necessary two-thirds majority needed for approval. The old Carnegie Library was still safe, and the city had an opportunity to rethink the plan for the new library. Instead, Council member Leslie Fisk, who led the drive for the failed $2.4 million bond plan, came up with a plan for a reduced $1.7 million bond issue, to be submitted to voters in April 1965.

Proponents of the new library stepped up their campaign efforts as the April election neared. The *Times-Herald* joined in those efforts, running an editorial describing the Carnegie Library as an "antiquated and all-but-falling-down monstrosity" and labeling opposition to the new library as "cantankerous rather than constructive." But this time, instead of missing the two-thirds majority by just a few percentage points the supporters of the new library lost badly—getting only 52 percent of all ballots cast.

Vallejo was at another crossroads. But even though voters had said "no" twice to the new library funding, Council members moved ahead with a lease-purchase plan, with lease payments to be covered by a three-cent increase in cigarette taxes. Sen. Gibson helped to obtain a $900,000 federal grant, and the eventual cost of the new building was $2.3 million. This time, voters didn't have a say in the process.

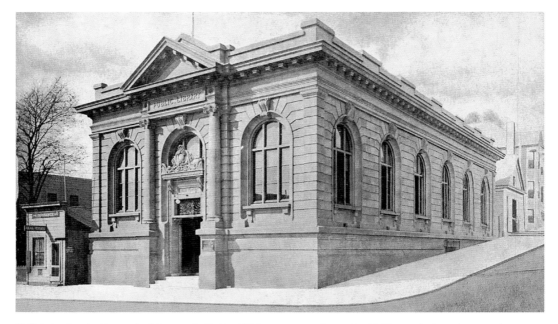

Vallejo's classic Carnegie Library, built in 1903, was torn down in 1970—a victim of a massive downtown redevelopment project that resulted in demolition of more than 500 old structures. (*Vallejo Naval and Historical Museum*)

Time was running out for the Carnegie Library. In August 1969, the redevelopment agency heard another plea to preserve the old structure and incorporate it into the Marina Vista project, possibly as a science building or museum for children. But the preservation proponents, Solano Junior College art instructor Dorothy Herger and interior designer Jeanette Lammel, were told by VRA Chairman Lowell Nelson that preservation wasn't an option. But he said the structure would be given to anyone willing to move the structure—an impossible task without major support.

A year later, in September 1970, the Carnegie Library was torn down after 65 years of service. At the time, local historian Ernie Wichels said the demolition was necessary because the old structure was "the most dangerous public building in town." Wichels said the building was made of non-reinforced brick covered by a stone facing, and would have collapsed in the event of a major earthquake. "It's a good thing no one tried to carry out a proposal of several months ago to move and relocate the old structure," an It's Rich column in the *Times-Herald* stated. "It wouldn't have made it across the street."

When a copper box in the cornerstone salvaged from the old library was opened, city officials found that photographs, newspapers, a chart of Mare Island Strait, a Sunrise Cemetery map, the rules for every fraternal order in Vallejo and other documents inside had deteriorated badly. The cornerstone, a fragment of a unique historical building that was lost forever, was to be mounted at the new 90,000-square-foot John F. Kennedy Library. However, the only cornerstone that's clearly visible now bears a 1969 date. The new library was dedicated on Oct. 3, 1970.

Heroic Rescue Effort Saved Shipwrecked USS *Saginaw* Crew (Sept. 15, 2019)

The saga of the ill-fated USS *Saginaw*, first of more than 500 ships built at Mare Island and the first Navy vessel launched on the West Coast, is as compelling as any shipwreck story you will ever read. Here's a brief retelling of that amazing tale.

Launched on March 3, 1859, the 155-foot-long, 460-ton side-wheeler was powered by sail and steam. The wooden sloop-of-war had patrolled waters from Panama to Alaska and also saw service along the coast of China before running aground and breaking up on a remote reef in the North Pacific Ocean in 1870.

The ship was sent in early 1870 to Midway Atoll, where a coal depot was to be built, as a support vessel for hard-hat divers who tried unsuccessfully to blast a wide channel through coral reefs to the atoll's lagoon. In October the blasting stopped and the *Saginaw* headed for Ocean Island, about 50 miles away, to make a routine check for any castaways before returning to San Francisco. The atoll, now called Kure Atoll, was a known shipwreck site and LCDR Montgomery Sicard, the *Saginaw*'s commanding officer, ordered that the ship move slowly at night under reduced steam and sails. He calculated that the ship would be near the atoll, in safe waters, by daybreak. But strong currents carried the ship onto outlying reefs shortly after 3 a.m. on Oct. 30, and before dawn the *Saginaw* was a shattered wreck.

Miraculously, all 93 men on board made it safely to shore—marooned on one of the most remote spots in the world. Kure Atoll, at the far northwest end of the Hawaiian Islands, is

The Mare Island-built USS *Saginaw* ran aground on a remote reef in the North Pacific Ocean in 1870. The castaways were finally rescued after five volunteers sailed and rowed a small boat 1,500 miles to Hawaii. (*Vallejo Naval and Historical Museum*)

about 1,400 miles from Honolulu, 3,200 miles from the California coast, 2,400 miles from Japan and 1,700 miles from the Aleutians. The atoll is a ring of coral encircling a lagoon and an island a mile long, a half-mile wide and no more than 20 feet above sea level.

Salvaged food was strictly rationed and the sailors were able to find a small source of underground water. They also ate monk seals, gooney birds (albatross), fish and sea turtles, and if necessary were prepared to eat rats that overran the island. They were surviving, but Sicard knew that no other ship might visit the island for months and food and water could run out. He ordered that his 26-foot captain's gig, an open rowing whaleboat, be fitted with sails. The boat was covered over with wood and canvas and two short masts with small sails were added. On Nov. 18, five volunteers set off on a dangerous 31-day voyage, rowing and sailing for about 1,500 miles. They all were alive when land was sighted, but only William Halford survived after the boat capsized in the surf near Hanalei Bay, Kauai. Halford, exhausted and half-starved, was able to wade ashore and find help. The captain of a local schooner changed his sailing plans and brought Halford to Honolulu, arriving on Christmas Eve. Halford rushed to the American consulate and within hours two rescue ships were headed to Kure Atoll, including the royal steamer *Kilauea* sent by King Kamehameha. The *Kilauea* reached the atoll on Jan. 3, 68 days after the shipwreck, and sent boats ashore the next day for the *Saginaw* castaways. Their ordeal was over.

Halford, a veteran sailor and survivor of at least two previous shipwrecks, was awarded the Congressional Medal of Honor and promoted from coxswain to gunner for his heroism. He retired as a chief gunner in August 1903. During World War I Halford was recalled to Navy duty as a lieutenant. In his 70s at that point, he was the Navy's oldest officer. He died Feb. 7, 1919, at age 77 and is buried in the Mare Island Cemetery.

Halford's great-grandson, Ralph Halford of Vallejo, has the Medal of Honor, along with old photographs, documents and other mementos. The Mare Island Museum's artifacts include Lt. Halford's sword. The Vallejo Naval and Historical Museum's collections include a small-scale model of the *Saginaw* and a large-scale model of the ship's bow. The *Saginaw*'s bell is on display at a center in Hilo, Hawaii; and a crude sextant used by the gig crew is among *Saginaw* artifacts at the U.S. Naval Academy in Annapolis. But the most significant artifact, the still-intact 26-foot rescue gig that reached Kauai in 1870, is in storage, in the hands of the Navy's History and Heritage Command in Washington, D.C.

"The story of the *Saginaw* itself is amazing, and the fact that the gig still exists is incredible," says Jim Kern, executive director of the Vallejo Naval and Historical Museum. The gig was returned to the Navy about three years ago from the Castle Museum in *Saginaw*, Mich. Before that, it was on display at the Naval Academy for many decades. In recent years, there have been discussions of requesting a loan of the gig on a long-term basis for Mare Island or the San Francisco Maritime National Park, although no formal requests are in the works now.

Many books and articles have been written about the *Saginaw*, including a 2017 book *The Wreck of the Saginaw* by Cornelia Bagg Srey and her son, Pyara Bagg Sandhu. They are in Sicard's family line. A 2010 book, *A Civil War Gunboat in Pacific Waters: Life on Board USS Saginaw*, was written by Hans Van Tilburg, who led the team that discovered the *Saginaw*'s remains in 2003. *The Last Cruise of the USS Saginaw*, written by the ship's paymaster, George H. Read, was published in 1912.

The USS *Jeannette* Disaster—Another Mare Island Story (Dec. 8, 2019)

In early 1879 Mare Island shipyard workers began transforming the USS *Jeannette*, a 146-foot, three-masted and steam-powered vessel, into what was described as the strongest, best-equipped ship for survival in crushing Arctic pack ice. But the *Jeannette*'s polar expedition that began later in the year ultimately ended in tragedy.

Extensive preparations included reinforcing the hull of the ship, a former Royal Navy gunboat, with internal double trusses and iron box beams. Its bow was filled in with solid timber and strengthened outside with stout elm planking and iron straps. Two new state-of-the-art boilers, a desalinization plant and new heating system were installed, interior spaces were insulated with thick felt, and the ship was packed with enough supplies to keep its crew of 33 men alive and healthy for three years.

On July 8, 1879, 10 days after a commissioning ceremony at Mare Island, the *Jeannette* headed out the Golden Gate on a U.S. Navy expedition financed by millionaire James Gordon Bennett Jr. The *New York Herald* tycoon hoped the ship would be the first in recorded history to reach the North Pole. Bennett had recently captured the world's attention by sending journalist Henry Morton Stanley to Africa to find Dr. David Livingstone, a famed explorer who had been searching for the source of the Nile River. He wanted to capitalize on that sensation with the *Jeannette*'s voyage.

The expedition began smoothly enough, but by early September the ship was caught in drifting sea ice about 100 nautical miles from Wrangel Island. The *Jeannette* raised steam and repeatedly charged the pack ice, trying to batter a way forward. A thick plume of smoke from its stack, observed by three whaling ships about 10 miles away, was the final sighting of the ship by the outside world. Shortly afterwards, the *Jeannette* was sealed within the pack "as tightly as a fly in amber" according to historian Leonard Guttridge, and remained stuck for 21 straight months. Finally, as shifting ice crushed the *Jeannette*'s hull, the crew abandoned ship. At about 4 a.m. on June 13, 1881, the *Jeannette* sank.

Stranded more than 700 miles from the North Pole and almost a thousand miles from the nearest landmass, the Arctic coast of central Siberia, the crew began a long, perilous journey across the ice to safety. Besides hauling tons of provisions, the sailors dragged three small boats that they boarded after reaching open water. Following short stays on a few islands they encountered, the explorers made a final run for the mainland. But a violent storm developed and one boat carrying eight men disappeared without a trace. The other two boats completed the crossing, reaching land at widely separated points after several days at sea. It was mid-September, three months after the *Jeannette* had gone under. Eleven men from one boat soon found some Siberian natives and were saved. But the 14 crew members from the other boat became lost on land, and only two of them survived. The dead included George Washington De Long, the *Jeannette*'s captain. In all, only 13 of the 33 crew members survived.

Author Hampton Sides, in his 2014 book *In the Kingdom of Ice: The Grand and Terrible Polar Voyage of the USS Jeannette*, described the horrors some of the men faced, including frostbite, crude amputations, madness and starvation. Writing about De Long's penchant for understatement in the face of all the hardships, Sides said, "Gazing at a puzzle of jammed ice and meltwater that would require weeks to cross, he stoically predicted: 'We are in for a time.' Hopelessly disoriented by fog for the better part of a week, De Long would only allow that 'we are in the dark as to our position.' Halted by a lashing blizzard, he scribbled that the day's weather was 'anything but satisfactory.'"

In 1869, Mare Island shipyard workers transformed USS *Jeannette* into what they figured would be the strongest, best-equipped ship for survival in crushing Arctic ice. (*Vallejo Naval and Historical Museum*)

When the first survivors began arriving home in the U.S. in May 1882 they were greeted as heroes. While their quest had been a failure, their story of survival and De Long's courage in keeping as many alive as he could cemented their place in the history of Arctic exploration. Two months earlier, searchers had found the frozen bodies of De Long and other members of the expedition who died after reaching Siberia. They also found De Long's notebook, with a final entry dated Oct. 30, 1881—140 days after the *Jeannette* had sunk. The bodies were brought back to the U.S. in 1883 for burial.

The disastrous *Jeannette* voyage, officially called the U.S. Arctic Expedition, was an attempt to reach the North Pole by pioneering a route from the Pacific Ocean through the Bering Strait. The premise was that a temperate current flowed northwards into the strait, providing a gateway to an open sea and the Pole. But the theory proved illusory. After the *Jeannette*'s voyage, Sides wrote, "No other Arctic explorer undertook an expedition with a serious intention of meeting an open polar sea."

Though they failed to reach the Pole, the *Jeannette* explorers did discover some new Arctic islands, one of which they named after Bennett, their wealthy and eccentric sponsor. The ship's meteorological and oceanographic records also provided climatologists with valuable data relating to climate change and the shrinking of the polar icecap.

In February 2015 the Russian adventurer, traveler and media personality Andrey Khoroshev announced that in consultation with the Russian Geographical Society, he would try to locate and raise the wreck of *Jeannette*, which may be down only about 60 feet. Since then, one survey of the area where the ship sank was conducted (Lat. N77.25, Long. E155) but it has not yet been found. Khoroshev said raising the ship wouldn't be difficult and that event would be a great boost for Russia's relations with the United States, "which are not very good right now."

4

2020 Columns

Mighty Midget Ships Had Key Role in WWII Battles (Jan. 19, 2020)

Small, heavily armed Navy gunboats, dubbed "Mighty Midgets," provided intense, life-saving cover fire for many U.S. Army soldiers, Marines and sailors during bloody amphibious assaults in World War II. The last of these little-known ships now is docked at Mare Island, serving as a floating museum that's open to the public.

The 158-foot-long, shallow-draft LCS (Landing Craft Support) ships were small compared with other Navy warships—less than half the length of a destroyer. But they more than made up for their size with their weaponry. Mare Island's "Midget" has a 3"/50-caliber gun mounted on the bow that could shoot an exploding projectile nearly nine miles. The ship also had two twin-mounted 40-mm anti-aircraft guns, four single-mounted 20-mm anti-aircraft guns, four .50-caliber machine guns, and 10 rocket launchers. The gunboats were the Navy's most heavily armed vessels per ton of displacement. Descriptions of the ships during battles include one comparing them to a lethal 4th of July fireworks show.

About 10,000 sailors served aboard 130 "Mighty Midgets" during WWII, including Bill Mason, 93, who is the skipper of LCS(L)(3)102 at Mare Island. He was a teen-age sailor aboard another "Midget" during the war—and is the only one of its 71 crew members still alive.

Mason has vivid WWII memories, including the battle of Okinawa, the largest amphibious landing and bloodiest battle in the Pacific theater. His ship was repeatedly targeted by Japanese kamikaze planes, including two he shot down while manning one of the 20-mm guns. He and other volunteers on the only still-intact "Midget" now face a struggle in preserving it as a memorial to all the LCS sailors and their contributions to the Allied victory.

Mason and the ship's executive officer, Gordon Stutrud, say there's uncertainty about its future due to costs of maintenance and berthing space—and the ability of an aging crew of volunteers to keep up with needed work. They also wonder how their ship and parent Landing Craft Support Museum, a 501(c)(3) now on the National Register of Historic Places, will mesh with the vision of the Nimitz Group, the new owners of the former Mare Island Naval Shipyard.

Small, heavily armed navy ships, dubbed "Mighty Midgets," helped to achieve U.S. victories during critical WWII beach-head assaults. Only one of the ships still exists, tied up at Mare Island. (*Vallejo Naval and Historical Museum*)

Mason hopes for positive news in upcoming meetings with Nimitz Group executives. "This is Navy history—75 years of it," he says. "We'd like to get some kind of arrangement that we can afford and that will ensure we can stay open to the public." The ship was commissioned in early 1945, and an event is scheduled for Feb. 15 in honor of its 75th year afloat this year.

Plans for the "Mighty Midgets" were drawn up by military leaders who realized they had to do something to reduce high U.S. death rates during WWII beach-head assaults. One of the worst losses—about 1,800 U.S. troops—occurred during the Nov. 20–23, 1943, Battle of Tarawa. But it wasn't until 1944 and 1945 that 130 LCS gunboats were launched. With their heavy firepower, the 387-ton ships had a critical role in amphibious assaults at the close of the war.

The "Mighty Midgets" saw combat at Iwo Jima, Okinawa, the Philippines, Borneo and elsewhere in the Pacific. A standard battle tactic for the gunboats was a first assault on an enemy beach, getting within 500 yards while firing rocket barrages. On successive runs, they would be followed by landing craft that would pass by them to reach the beaches. The LCS gunboats would keep firing over the heads of the U.S. troops who were wading ashore, protecting them against enemy fire.

With an anchor attached to 900 feet of cable on the stern of the gunboats, crews also could drop anchor offshore, run their ship onto beaches for close fire support, and then drag the ship off the beach by winching in the cable. Other tasks included "skunk patrol," intercepting Japanese suicide boats that were trying to ram Navy ships; and service as picket ships to help spot and shoot down incoming bombers and smaller kamikaze planes. It was dangerous duty: From late January to mid-July, 1945, 26 of the gunboats were sunk or heavily damaged.

The "Midgets" had no names—only a string of letters and numbers. But the crew of the one remaining LCS at Mare Island gave their ship an unofficial name of "Yankee Dollar," from the lyrics of a popular song of the day, "Rum and Coca Cola" by the Andrew Sisters.

Following WWII, surviving LCS ships returned to the United States. Many were transferred to Japan, France, Vietnam, Cambodia, Thailand, Greece and other nations, and some underwent major modifications and became fishing boats. In 1953 LCS-102 was turned over to the Japanese Navy and renamed the JDS Himawari. In 1966 the ship went to the Royal Thailand Navy and renamed the HTMS Nakha. By the early 2000s, the Nakha was out of service and resting on a mudbank. Mason, who became a professor of economics and had a long career in California's state college and university system, spearheaded a decade-long effort to get the ship back to the states. Finally, in 2007 it was loaded onto a commercial heavy-lift cargo vessel and brought here.

The Navy's "Midgets" weren't built at Mare Island. However, the shipyard made a major contribution to the WWII amphibious assault effort, assembling 301 LCTs (Landing Craft-Tank) during the war, and Mason says the old shipyard was his "first realistic choice" for what he hopes will be the final homeport for "Yankee Dollar."

Squatter-Settler Conflicts Led to Vigilante Murder (Feb. 2, 2020)

Arguments over property and poultry led to an 1863 vigilante murder by disguised men who repeatedly shot a well-known Vallejo farmer and racetrack owner who had just been arrested for shooting and wounding another man. Many residents knew the killers—but nobody was ever convicted.

Manuel Vera, 34, a native of Portugal who had been in Vallejo since the mid-1850s, was shot 17 times by men who wore masks or blackened their faces to hide their identities. Depending on what old news account you read, a Solano County sheriff's deputy guarding Vera either had just left for a few minutes to get dinner or backed off when confronted by 60 to 100 armed men who rode horseback down Georgia Street in search of Vera.

The lynch mob murder was part of a wave of violence in California during an early-statehood period of uncertainty over land ownership that prompted squatters to build shacks on property that had been part of sprawling Spanish and Mexican land grants, ignoring original or new owners' demands to leave.

Vera and his half-brother Elias Viera were among the new landowners. Between the two men, by mid-1861 they had bought more than 100 acres on the east edge of town, along what's now Springs Road just east of Interstate 80. The land was sold by John Frisbie, who was parceling out part of the 84,000-acre Rancho Suscol grant from the Mexican government to his father-in-law, Gen. Mariano Vallejo.

Vera decided in December 1861 to rent part of the farm to the Preston family, taking in exchange a share of their crops and some chickens. But in a September 1862 confrontation, he demanded more chickens than the Prestons wanted to hand over. That started a fight that ended with Bill Preston shooting Vera. He survived, but the Prestons were still squatting on his land. He also faced an assault charge that eventually was dismissed.

In 1863, vigilantes rode horseback into downtown Vallejo, cornered Manuel Vera, who had been arrested for wounding a squatter, and riddled him with bullets. There were no convictions for the murder. (*Vallejo Naval and Historical Museum*)

Then, in early May 1863, Bill Preston and a man named Shafley were walking near the farm when a gunman in a wheat field fired a shot, wounding Shafley. Vera was arrested, on the belief that he intended to shoot Preston and hit Shafley instead. Angry friends of the two men threatened to retaliate by killing Vera and there was no secure jail in Vallejo, so Sheriff John Neville planned to take him to the Mare Island shipyard. But by dusk on May 6 Vera was still in downtown Vallejo, being held temporarily in prominent Vallejo merchant E.J. Wilson's family apartment, on the second floor of the Wilson Building on the northwest corner of Georgia and Sacramento streets.

"The shades of night were hardly closed when the mounted band of squatters rode into town like a company of soldiers," Frank Leach, founder of the *Vallejo Chronicle*, stated in his *Recollections of a Newspaperman* book. Some men held the horses and it didn't take the others very long to invade the apartment, "find Vera and riddle his body with bullets," Leach wrote.

A *Daily Alta California* account said the gunmen "murdered Vera, by firing their weapons coward-like, through the door of his room. After some dozen shots they plucked up courage enough to enter the room, where they found their victim still alive, and they dispatched him."

"On examination, it was found that some nine or ten balls or shot had entered Vera's heart. The reason assigned, for the cowardly nature of the assassination was that Vera was a brave and determined man, who might escape even from a dozen armed men, who might attempt his life."

Vera was buried in St. Vincent Cemetery. An inscription on his gravestone reads, "May God forgive my persecutors." His property, sold at an estate auction, included

40 horses, among them two thoroughbred race horses, many acres of wheat to be harvested, buggies, wagons, saddles, hogs, chickens, all sorts of farm equipment, 20 tons of hay, and household furniture—in all "a rare and splendid chance for farmers, housekeepers and sportsmen," an auction ad stated.

In early June Gov. Leland Stanford offered an $800 reward for information about the murderers. The reward was increased by $2,500 by the sheriff, who may have received a pledge of funds from Vera's estate. Finally, a grand jury took up the case and 17 men were indicted in mid-December. The sheriff, fearing more bloodshed if the indicted men resisted arrest, sought help and a cavalry company, the Suisun Light Dragoons, was ordered by the governor to round up the suspects. News accounts named the men as brothers Bill and F.A. Preston, Hugh and Thomas Magrain, Job G. Wean, A. G. Ripley, P. S. Schaeffer, Cor. Martin, Thomas Potter, Charles Winegar, Samuel Brown, John Hurley, Thomas Kidean, Newton Gwin, George Hunter, Levi Whitney, and a man listed by his last name, Ross.

Vera's family hoped for justice, but it wasn't forthcoming. The indicted men were to be tried separately, starting in January 1864 with F. A. Preston who was represented by N. Green Curtis, a prominent Sacramento criminal defense attorney. Curtis argued Preston wasn't clearly identified as one of the shooters, and his Fairfield trial ended after several days with a "not guilty" verdict. The Vallejo Chronicle reported that prosecutors considered the trial a test case and decided to drop the charges against other defendants, figuring their trials also would end with "not guilty" verdicts.

Forty-five years later, a history column in the Vallejo paper concluded with words that have stood the test of time. Describing the 1864 reaction to the verdict, the article stated: "What the people who were not biased thought about it is about the same as those of the present day will think after reading the account of it."

Solano County's Japanese Sent to Internment Camps in WWII (March 1, 2020)

The California Assembly formally apologized on Feb. 20 for helping the U.S. government imprison West Coast Japanese Americans in internment camps during World War II. Those sent to the remote camps included more than 1,000 men, women and children of Japanese descent who were living in Solano County.

The state Assembly's action followed Gov. Gavin Newsom's Feb. 19 declaration of a Day of Remembrance—the day in 1942 when President Franklin Roosevelt signed Executive Order 9066 that forced more than 120,000 people to 10 camps in the West and in Arkansas.

A congressional commission concluded in 1983 that the detentions, which started soon after Japan's Dec. 7, 1941, attack on Pearl Harbor, stemmed from "racial prejudice, war hysteria and failure of political leadership." In 1988, the U.S. government apologized and authorized $20,000 apiece to claimants. Payments eventually totaled $1.6 billion.

Even before Roosevelt's order was issued, authorities were making arrests in Vallejo, designated a "forbidden zone" because of its proximity to the Navy's Mare Island shipyard. That included nine arrests on Feb. 6 at two Japanese-operated businesses, the Navy Laundry at 411 York St. and the New Frisco Café at 203 Georgia St.

Most Japanese Americans from Solano County who were sent to internment camps during WWII were held at the Gila River camp in the Arizona desert. (*Vallejo Naval and Historical Museum*)

The Vallejo round-up was termed a wartime necessity to protect Mare Island. Nat Pieper, director of the San Francisco FBI office, said the raids were conducted because of "very definite suspicions of espionage." In a Dec. 21, 1941, editorial, the *Vallejo Times-Herald* said any aid to the enemy had to be stopped by "whatever means necessary—including concentration camps."

On Feb. 24, the *Times-Herald* reported that about 130 "enemy aliens" in the Vallejo area had been ordered to move. There was an early focus on Vallejo and also on Benicia because of their U.S. military bases, but most of the Solano County detainees were involved in farming and other businesses in Suisun, Fairfield and Vacaville areas. Some Japanese families had been there since the late 1800s, and more than half of those sent to the camps were born in the U.S. The rushed move to the camps resulted in many losing much or all of their property.

"Time was short," Takashi Tsujita wrote about his WWII experiences as a Vacaville teenager. "Our families did what they could to store or sell cars, refrigerators, washing machines and other household goods. Many items sold for 10 cents on the dollar. Much was simply given away."

Alice Otsuji Hager of Vallejo, in a 2001 *Times-Herald* article, said she was living in Napa on her family's farm, but the family was forced to leave and lost the property. "We never got a penny for it," she said. "All the farm equipment just disappeared. We were raped—figuratively speaking."

Accounts of raids, arrests, contraband seizures and internment preparations were front-page news at first. But on May 2–3, 1942, weekend when most of the detainees boarded trains and buses in Vacaville, the *Times-Herald* ran only brief accounts on inside pages. Another brief story ran in the Vallejo Evening News on the following Monday.

Living standards at the camps were never much above a bare subsistence level. Barracks were divided so that a family typically occupied a single 20-by-25-foot room. Barbed wire was strung around most of the camps, and entrances were controlled by guards. Most of the people from Solano County were first sent to temporary facilities in Turlock and Tulare and then to the Gila River "relocation center" in the Arizona desert.

Vallejo native Charles Kikuchi joined his family at Tanforan, a Bay Area peninsula racetrack converted into a temporary camp. "I understand we are going to live in the horse stalls," he wrote. "I hope the Army has the courtesy to remove the manure first." Horse stalls also were converted to temporary housing at the Turlock fairgrounds. After about four months, the Kikuchis went to the Gila River camp.

Of the estimated 120,000-plus detainees, about 54,000 returned to the West Coast after the war. Others relocated to other states, and nearly 5,000 returned to Japan. The last of the camps closed in March 1946.

Some returning to former communities faced difficulties. In Solano County, resolutions opposing their return came from county supervisors, the Vacaville Chamber of Commerce and the Vacaville chapter of the American Legion. But public attitudes were significantly improved by combat records of Japanese American soldiers, most of them with families in the camps.

The 442nd Regimental Combat Team, mostly second-generation American soldiers of Japanese ancestry (Nisei), became the most decorated unit in U.S. military history for its size and length of service. The unit, combined with the all-Nisei 100th Infantry Battalion, earned more than 18,000 awards during WWII, including 9,486 Purple Hearts. Twenty-one of its members were awarded Medals of Honor.

A partial list of soldiers from Solano County who were in the regiment includes Hisami "Sam" Yoshihara, George Noguchi and George Handa from Vacaville; Teruo Miyagishima of Fairfield; Dane Kato, Henry Maeyama and Kazuo Muto, from the Suisun area. Many other Nisei from the county served in the U.S. military during the war. They included Dye Ogata of Vallejo and Suisun brothers Grant and Tomio Ichikawa, all honored for their WWII duty in the Military Intelligence Service.

"Americans should study what we did because even right after the war we returned to the West Coast and the locals were still against us and would shoot our barns and try to chase us away again," Grant Ichikawa stated at a 2010 Washington, D.C., event honoring patriotism of Japanese Americans soldiers during the war. "That all changed probably because of the service we gave in the Pacific and European Theater."

Vallejo Helped 1906 SF Quake Victims (April 12, 2020)

Vallejo citizens and Mare Island sailors and Marines stepped up in a big way 114 years ago when San Francisco was hit by a massive 7.9 magnitude earthquake and firestorms that killed an estimated 3,000 people and destroyed about 28,000 buildings.

The earthquake struck at 5:12 a.m. on April 18, 1906, causing damage but no deaths in Vallejo. Telegraph and telephone lines were knocked down, so news of the much more extensive destruction in San Francisco didn't reach Vallejo or the Mare Island shipyard

Rear Adm. Bowman McCalla (left), commandant of Mare Island Naval Shipyard, and Vallejo Mayor J. J. Madigan led efforts by the shipyard and by the town of Vallejo to help victims of the 1906 San Francisco earthquake. (*Vallejo Naval and Historical Museum*)

until two hours later. First word came from the crew of a Navy launch that had departed from the city immediately after the quake, and more information came from terrified survivors who arrived in Vallejo about 9 a.m. on a ferryboat from San Francisco.

The roles of Vallejo and Mare Island Naval Shipyard in providing assistance, detailed by Thomas Lucy in a December 1992 Solano Historian account, began the day of the quake with Navy vessels steaming to San Francisco and Vallejo Mayor J. J. Madigan forming a relief committee headed by prominent attorney Frank Devlin.

Also, Zephaniah Jefferson Hatch, co-owner of the local Monticello Steamship Co., offered free use of the Monticello steamer to deliver emergency supplies and bring back refugees. Several other ferries also transported quake victims and by the end of April more than 2,500 people were in temporary shelters in Vallejo, a town of about 12,000 residents in 1906. Many of the homeless went to a tent camp in City Park or to the Vallejo Pavilion, a skating rink at Georgia and Sutter streets that doubled as a hub for various civic events. Others were placed in private homes around town, and temporary housing also was arranged in South Vallejo and in Glen Cove.

Rear Adm. Bowman McCalla, Mare Island shipyard commandant, ordered that the Naval YMCA in downtown Vallejo be used as a hospital and also directed the USS *Preble*, captained by Lt. Frederick Freeman, and other Navy ships, tugs and fireboats to deliver medical teams and to help fight rapidly spreading fires. The sailors were credited with saving important areas of San Francisco's waterfront from destruction.

Marines from Mare Island also helped to fight fires and provide security, and Navy ships transported many victims to safety.

Most refugees who poured into Vallejo were welcomed, but it was a different story for about 200 Chinese who arrived by ferry the day after the quake. In his 1992 account, Thomas Lucy said the city's relief committee "did not know what to do." The dilemma, which stemmed from strong anti-Chinese prejudice in the U.S., was resolved by local merchant Ah Fong Soon, known as the "king of the Chinese in Vallejo." He set up a segregated camp on Benicia Road and asked only for some hay for bedding and sacks of flour from the city relief group.

City trustees also heard complaints that some Vallejo businesses, including some restaurants, jacked up their prices during the crisis, so they ordered a rollback to pre-earthquake prices and threatened to revoke licenses of any business that didn't comply with the order.

There were several cases of lost children, including a newborn baby abandoned on one Vallejo-bound ferryboat and taken in by Alfred "Alf" and Sarah Edgecumbe. After trying for a year to find the parents, the Edgecumbes adopted the baby and named her Lodena. Growing up, she showed talent as a dancer and wound up touring with dance companies around the world. Lodena returned to Vallejo in 1933 and opened a dance studio here, becoming a teacher and mentor for hundreds—possibly thousands—of Vallejo youths.

As part of Vallejo's relief effort, Dr. Robert Dempsey organized a corps of 50 nurses and 50 stretcher-bearers to help bring badly injured people here for medical care. "We did amputations, attended badly burned and mangled people, set a hundred or so factures (without x-ray), and did quite a number of cranial (compressions) where cornices and bricks had fallen on the heads of people as they rushed from the indoors onto the streets," he said in a 1947 talk to medical students.

Dempsey also said the catastrophe led to establishment of Vallejo's first hospital at 502 Virginia St., now the site of the First United Methodist Church. Dempsey said Dr. James Hogan bought an old rooming house, The Wadsworth, which stood there at the time and turned it into the precursor of Vallejo General Hospital. Prior to the quake, the Navy's hospital on Mare Island was the only one in the immediate area.

Refugees not laid up with injuries were eager to find work, and Mayor Madigan, backed by former mayors James Roney and P. B. Lynch, sought federal funds so that Mare Island could hire more employees. President Theodore Roosevelt immediately endorsed the plan and on April 30 a $100,000 emergency appropriation was approved by Congress. The next day the shipyard began hiring nearly 400 new workers. Private industry got involved too, notably the Suisun Cement Co. which on May 5 told the relief committee it had more than 100 job openings.

Some refugees decided to set up their own businesses in Vallejo. They included David Beronio, who had been a master chef at the Palace Hotel in San Francisco. In his new town, he started a barber shop and other ventures and raised a son, also named David Beronio, who years later became a widely known sports writer and editor for Vallejo newspapers. It's not known how many other refugees became permanent Vallejo residents.

Those who found refuge in Vallejo showed their appreciation in various ways. The Alvarez family—parents and six children—found a temporary home with a local family and while there a seventh child was born. To honor the town and the Monticello steamship that brought the family here, the baby boy was named Vallejo Monticello Alvarez.

"That was one occasion when Vallejo went all out and did a magnificent job," Dr. Dempsey recalled. "No one lacked for food, clothes or housing. All of us had a household full of involuntary guests and we certainly enjoyed the privilege and did our best. Such happenings bring out the best in human nature."

Navy Beaches Sub, Cruiser on NorCal Coast (July 5, 2020)

A U.S. Navy submarine running on the surface and lost in pea-soup fog ran aground near Eureka, Calif., in late 1916. Bungled salvage efforts a month later led to the loss of a $7 million cruiser sent from Mare Island to tow the sub back to sea. At the time it was the Navy's worst peacetime disaster.

The Dec. 14 beaching of the submarine *H-3*, also known as the USS *Garfish*, and destruction of the USS *Milwaukee* amounted to a tragic case of "whatever can go wrong will go wrong," starting with the fog-bound sub. Crewmembers caught a glimpse of a smoke stack and aimed for it, thinking it was the stack of its mother ship, the USS

A navy submarine ran aground near Eureka, California, in 1916, and the disaster got much worse when a $7 million cruiser sent from Mare Island to drag the sub off the beach also ran aground. (*Vallejo Naval and Historical Museum*)

Cheyenne, in safe waters. But it was a shore-side stack of the Hammond Lumber Co., and the 150-foot-long sub ran aground, broadside in dangerous surf at Samoa Beach, just north of the narrow entrance to Humboldt Bay.

The *Cheyenne*, commanded by Cmdr. W. B. Howe, and three subs, the *H-1*, *H-2* and *H-3*, had left Bremerton, Wash., earlier in the month and were headed down the Northern California coast—in a hazardous area known as the "graveyard of the Pacific" because its rough seas and foggy weather had caused many shipwrecks. The plan was to enter the bay and get information on its possible future use by Navy submarines.

Coast Guard sailors stationed near the beach managed to rig ropes to the rolling sub and, aided by local residents, pulled the 27 *H-3* crew members ashore, one at a time. They used a breeches buoy, a life ring with a leg harness attached to a line that could be drawn back and forth from the sub to the shore. The last man to reach shore was the sub captain, Lt. Harry Bogusch, 14 hours after the vessel ran aground. Several thousand people gathered to watch the rescues.

The Navy then sought bids from salvage companies to get the *H-3* back into the water. Mercer-Fraser Co., a Eureka contracting and engineering firm that still exists today, offered to do the work for $18,000, but the Navy thought it was too small an amount to be taken seriously—a big mistake, as it turned out. The only other bid, for $150,000, was rejected as too high. The Navy decided to attempt the salvage on its own, dispatching the *Milwaukee* from Mare Island where it had undergone a major overhaul.

The officer in charge of the effort to get the *H-3* off the beach was Lt. William F. Newton, temporarily in command of the *Milwaukee*. Ironically, Newton had been in command of the *H-3* when it ran aground off Point Sur in June 1915. Never a captain of anything bigger than a sub, he now was responsible for a 426-foot-long, 10,000-ton ship. Despite warnings from local mariners, Newton was determined to use the *Milwaukee* to tow the *H-3* to deep water. To help hold a course straight to sea and overcome a strong southerly current that would sweep any vessel toward land, lines ran from the ship to two smaller Navy vessels, the *Cheyenne* that was headed seaward and a Mare Island tug, the *Iroquois*, headed north.

"The plan worked on paper," says Eureka historian Raymond W. Hillman, who wrote a book about the fiasco, entitled *Shipwrecked at Samoa, California: The Loss of the Navy Cruiser USS Milwaukee*. But the plan failed as the *Milwaukee*, less than 600 yards from shore, raised anchor and put tension on a heavy steel cable linking the ship to the beached *H-3*. At that point the *Cheyenne*'s propeller slashed its Manila tow line to the cruiser, and sailors on the *Iroquois*, about to run aground, used axes to quickly cut their tow line. But the *Milwaukee* couldn't power to sea because the crew had no fast way to release its heavy steel tow cable—a major planning mistake. Leashed inescapably to the sub, the ship swung slowly to the south and into the surf zone. At 4:10 a.m. on Jan. 13, 1917, the cruiser, with a 24-foot draft, was in 12 feet of water, hard aground broadside to the beach and tilting at a 20-degree list—a helpless hulk.

Breeches buoys were used at first to get the crew off the doomed ship, followed by surfboats rowed by Coast Guard sailors and volunteers. It took until 8:30 p.m. to bring more than 400 men ashore. Lt. Newton was in the last surfboat. The next day, crewmen returned to the *Milwaukee* to retrieve $128,000 that had been left on a table in the officers' wardroom. Three days later, 270 men left on a special train for Mare Island, while remaining sailors stayed behind to salvage what they could from the ship. More than a century later, some wreckage from the *Milwaukee* can still be seen at very low tide.

On Jan. 17, James Fraser of the Mercer-Fraser company got word that the Navy had second thoughts and accepted the company's bid of $18,000 to salvage the *H-3* submarine. By late March, the sub was raised out of the sand, hauled 325 feet from the water line to dry sand and then cradled between two huge logs to hold her upright. A timber track was built and a donkey engine was used to haul the sub across a three-quarter-mile-wide sand spit to a Humboldt Bay launch site. On April 20, the sub was refloated and, after an extensive overhaul, remained in service until decommissioning in 1922. The sub was scrapped in 1931.

A formal Navy inquiry was expected. Besides the high dollar value of the lost cruiser and damage to the *H-3*, *Milwaukee* sailor H. F. Parker drowned when one of the surfboats overturned. Also, William Donnelly, a Mercer-Fraser worker, died in a fall from a trestle built from the shore to the *Milwaukee* to help in the salvage efforts. Historian Lynwood Carranco, who wrote extensively about the disaster, mentioned unverified reports that Lt. Newton was exonerated and Cmdr. Howe was hit with a reduction in grade. But Hillman says any impetus for a major inquiry would have faded with the nation's declaration of war against Germany in early April 1917 and corresponding U.S. military build-up. Any officers to blame for any Humboldt Bay screw-ups were urgently needed elsewhere in the Navy's World War I efforts.

Famed Author Got His Start in Vallejo (Aug. 2, 2020)

This column is about Ernest J. Gaines, who as a Black teenager in the late 1940s moved from the segregated Deep South to Vallejo, where the town's diversity, integrated schools and old Carnegie Library helped him on his path to become an internationally acclaimed author.

Gaines, who died late last year at age 86, always mentioned his five years in Vallejo, from age 15 in 1948 to age 20 in 1953, when asked about his life and brilliant writing about race, community and culture in rural south Louisiana where he was born. Without his time in Vallejo, Gaines repeatedly said he probably would not have achieved such literary success.

Gaines' first try at a book, at age 16, was rejected by a New York publisher and in disgust he burned the manuscript in his backyard. But his determination to write never left him. Ultimately, he wrote 10 books, including four novels that were made into films: *The Autobiography of Miss Jane Pittman*, *The Sky is Gray*, *A Gathering of Old Men*, and *A Lesson Before Dying*. His many awards and honors included the National Humanities Medal and nominations for a Pulitzer Prize and a Nobel Prize in Literature. He was the first writer-in-residence at the University of Louisiana at Lafayette, where the Ernest J. Gaines Center is now located.

Here are some quotes from Gaines that describe how his Vallejo years affected him. Most are from a 2019 book, *Ernest J. Gaines: Conversations*, edited by Marcia Gaudet.

When his mother and step-father, who had come to Vallejo in 1945, sent for him in 1948, Gaines said he attended schools "in a completely integrated area. I lived in government projects (Carquinez Heights), and a lot of the poorer people lived in those projects at that time, just after the war. My classmates and my playmates around the recreation center and on the playing fields were of different nationalities. Asians,

Ernest J. Gaines moved from the segregated Deep South to Vallejo in the late 1940s. He often said the town's diversity, integrated schools, and old Carnegie Library helped him to achieve fame as a prominent American author. (*David Humphreys photo*)

Hispanics, whites, the blacks. I got a chance to get around and be with people, much—so different than the experience I had in the South, where everything was white and black. There were no other groups. Whites here, blacks there."

Born at River Lake Plantation in the small town of Oscar, La., Gaines says, "I knew about the swamps; I knew about hunting. I knew about fishing. I used to fish in the bayous, in the river. I picked cotton, cut sugarcane. I knew all of these things before I went to California. I learned a lot. But I think if I'd have stayed in Louisiana for another five years until I was 20 or 21 years old, I think I could have been destroyed as so many of my contemporaries were. They no longer went further into education. They became quite bitter about their situations."

In Vallejo, Gaines' stepfather, Raphael Colar, was concerned because Gaines was hanging out on the streets after school. "I had to get off the block or else I was going to get myself in trouble, because the town where we lived was a Navy town, and a lot of sailors, a lot of bars, a lot of all kinds of things going on." He was told to go to the movies, the YMCA or the library. With no money for the movies, he went to the YMCA. That lasted a few weeks, "until I got in a ring with a guy who knew how to box, and that guy really beat me up. So I went to the library."

Vallejo's now-gone Andrew Carnegie Library, at Sacramento and Virginia streets, was the first library Gaines had entered. "I was not allowed in the public library in Louisiana, in the area where I lived," he said. "There were public libraries for African

Americans in the cities, Baton Rouge and New Orleans or places like that, but they were not very big libraries. But in the little town where I lived, there was no library there at all that I could attend." The library was only a few blocks from his second Vallejo home, at 219A Florida St., and Gaines was amazed at the all the books he could take out. He read French and Russian writers who described peasants in their own countries, and came across other authors as well. But not seeing his people from southern Louisiana in those books, he was inspired to write about them.

Gaines graduated from Franklin Junior High School in 1949, from Vallejo High in 1951 and from Vallejo Junior College in 1953. Franklin classmate Pearl Jones Tranter recalls Gaines' personality as "Coolness. Calm. Quiet. Didn't fidget. Didn't vie with others for attention. Paid attention to the teachers." Besides all his reading and writing, Gaines—"Ernie" to his friends—was active in sports throughout his school years. He said he was no good at football but was proud of his ability as a sprinter. His Vallejo Junior College record for the 220-yard dash stood for 20 years.

In 1953 Gaines joined the Army and spent two years in the service, including a year in Guam. After that, he enrolled at San Francisco State College, graduating in 1957. In 1958 he won a Wallace Stegner Creative Writing Fellowship to Stanford University and in 1964 published his first novel, Catherine Carmier. To make ends meet early in his writing career, he worked at various part-time jobs, including stints as a mail clerk and printer's devil. From the start, Gaines adhered to a discipline that he called his six golden rules of writing: "Read, read, read. Write, write, write." He lived in San Francisco for many years but eventually returned to his hometown of Oscar. There, he and his wife, Dianne Saulney-Gaines, built a home on part of the old plantation where he was born, and where his ancestors had lived since slavery. That's where he died on Nov. 5, 2019.

Town's First Woman Cop Was Tough—With Heart of Gold (Aug. 30, 2020)

Rose Rachel Milestein, the first woman to be issued a Vallejo police badge, was hired in 1944 and developed a reputation over a 20-year career as a fearless cop who was tough-minded but always ready to help women in desperate circumstances.

"Sister Rose," who combined her police work with Salvation Army volunteer activity that spanned about 40 years, patrolled Vallejo's notorious Lower Georgia Street sailor district during its worst years, when it was known for rampant boozing, gambling and prostitution.

The late Gordon Darling, Milestein's nephew, recalled in a 2008 *Times-Herald* story how he once got a call from a woman who had been working as a prostitute but whose life changed for the better when Milestein loaned her $5 and told her to leave town or face arrest.

"Rose would pick up the girls, give them $5, and put them on a Greyhound bus to go back home. She would tell them if they came back she would take them to jail," Darling said. "Years after Rose died, I got a call from this woman who wanted to meet me to pay back the $5 Rose had given her."

Frank Darling, Gordon's son and Milestein's great-nephew, recalls how his father would get late-night calls from his aunt because she needed to help someone who wasn't

Rose Milestein, the first woman to get a Vallejo police badge, earned a reputation as a tough cop always ready to help desperate women. (*Vallejo Naval and Historical Museum*)

within walking distance. Gordon was her go-to driver on her off-duty hours because she never owned a car. Milestein didn't need one to get to Vallejo's downtown police station—it was only a block from her flat on Carolina Street.

"Rose felt that it was her job to make sure women weren't getting into serious trouble," Darling said. "I heard stories from my father about her getting girls into safe havens even if that meant putting them in jail. If a woman had been beat up or was sick or trapped in something bad, she would do whatever she could to help them. She got my dad involved in so many things. She'd say, 'Gordon, it's the right thing to do.' And he would do what she asked. She was his surrogate mother."

"She was a tough-acting person, a cold, no-nonsense kind of person, but she was very helpful and would do anything for anybody."

Milestein was born in 1899 in Bucharest, Romania, which was under the pre-revolution Czarist Russian regime. During the revolution, her grandparents were killed and her family fled the country, first going to England and then to the United States and Canada. As a young woman, she joined the Salvation Army and for several years was a missionary in Hawaii. She married there and had a daughter, but the marriage didn't last and she returned to the mainland, coming to Vallejo in 1927. Milestein then attended a bible college in Texas and opened her own mission in St. Louis, Mo.

Historian Lee Fountain, in a 1997 *Solano Historian* account, says Milestein returned to the West Coast in 1936, arriving with her daughter by bus in Vallejo. Out of money, she connected with the Salvation Army here. In 1939 she was naturalized in Fairfield as a U.S. citizen, and during World War II got a job as a shipfitter's helper on Mare Island Naval Shipyard. Toward the end of the war Milestein passed a Civil Service test for the position of police matron. After she was hired, the position was reclassified as policewoman.

"It was not long before she became a familiar figure on the streets of Vallejo's waterfront," Fountain wrote. "She often patrolled the area alone at night, sometimes getting physically involved when alcohol, sailors and women of easy virtue were joined in celebration or combat. It is reported that she had been on the receiving end of a misdirected punch thrown by combatants fighting in the bars on Lower Georgia Street."

Milestein "saw the very seamy, sordid side of life of street characters, but it did not make her cynical or discouraged," Fountain added. "She once said, 'I've never met a really bad girl or a bad fellow who didn't have a spark of decency somewhere.'"

During the war, Milestein helped hundreds of young women, many of them homeless, without friends or funds, or unable to hold jobs. She organized groups that met at the Salvation Army headquarters on Sacramento Street, including a Junior Home League for barmaids and waitresses working in the Lower Georgia Street district. She didn't wear a police uniform but did carry a gun—which she never fired, according to Frank Darling.

Milestein received many honors for her professional and volunteer service, including "Woman of the Year" awards from the American Legion and from the Vallejo Business and Professional Women's Club. She also was cited for distinguished service by the National Police Officers Association of America and served as vice-president of the Women Peace Officers' Association of California.

At one community event held to honor her, then-Police Chief Jack Stiltz said, "Sister Rose does more good than all the rest of us put together."

Milestein faced mandatory retirement when she reached age 65 in 1964. But the Police Department gave her a year's extension until May 1965. After retiring she moved to Los Angeles and died there on May 2, 1969.

Rampant Crime in Vallejo's Long-Gone "Tule Town" (Sept. 27, 2020)

Vallejo's Lower Georgia Street sailor district was bulldozed flat a half-century ago but many people remember it or have heard about its numerous bars, casinos, bordellos and flophouses. All but forgotten was another high-crime district a few blocks away that existed in the late 1800s and early 1900s, predating Lower Georgia Street's notorious heyday.

The area was known as "Tule Town" because it was swampy land along a now-reclaimed stretch of the Napa River. Most of the illicit activity was in the 400 and 500 blocks of Pennsylvania Street, between Sonoma and Napa streets. A few more brothels, described as "female boarding" houses on 1901 Sanborn fire-insurance maps on file at the Vallejo Naval and Historical Museum, were located on nearby streets. In all, the Sanborn maps show 15 of the so-called boarding houses as well as several dance halls and saloons in a few blocks.

Tule Town was going strong when Dr. Robert Dempsey began his long Vallejo medical practice in 1903. Years later, he wrote that in the early 1900s Vallejo "had 7,000 people, 140

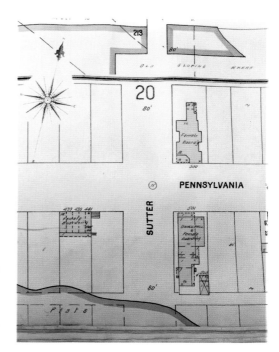

Early-day Vallejo maps depict saloons, dance halls and bordellos a few blocks from the town's once-notorious Lower Georgia Street sailor district. The high-crime area predated the heyday of Lower Georgia Street. (*Vallejo Naval and Historical Museum*)

saloons and it was said to have a prostitute population between 400 and 700." Besides Tule Town, the 100 and 200 blocks of Georgia Street—the center of Vallejo's notorious sailor district in World War II—were getting more bars, but in 1902 bars were far outnumbered by shops, markets, offices for newspapers and lawyers, doctors and other businesses.

In describing Tule Town, Dr. Dempsey wrote, "Here were hundreds of 'cribs,' a door and a window, opening onto a narrow board sidewalk elevated a few feet above the soupy mud of the so-called street. Every kind of pervert in the world inhabited those dens. Murders, beatings, robberies and other kinds of pernicious crimes were daily occurrences." While his "crib" count seems high given the number of permanent Tule Town buildings drawn on the Sanborn maps, it's possible that the map-makers ignored or weren't aware of smaller, ramshackle structures that had been nailed together in a hurry and would never qualify for fire insurance in the first place.

How did the doctor know so much about Tule Town? Dempsey's explanation was straightforward and simple: "The proprietors of these dens never called the police but generally sent for a doctor." Proprietors named in various news accounts about the area included William Caruthers, Dick Gray, Vivian Gordon, Laura Warde, Arthur Cloutier, George Cashmore, Charles Hamlin, Fred Martin and William Collins, among others.

"Once I was attacked by a Spanish woman with a stiletto because I would not give her cocaine," Dempsey said. "Fortunately, I was quicker than she and grabbed her wrist just as the needle-sharp stiletto put a hole in my Prince Albert coat, ripped my shirt and scratched my chest."

"Another time a sailor weighing 220 pounds and a great wrestler had D.T.s and hid behind a door. When I entered the room he grabbed me and I grabbed him. In the scuffle

I got a hammerlock on him and threw his shoulder out of joint. Needless to say, I got out of there as soon as possible. Such little things as these, with a lot more equally as tough, made life very interesting."

Tule Town definitely was a rough area. In February 1896 two San Francisco girls were rescued by constables from William Collins' brothel. The girls had responded to an ad in the *San Francisco Examiner* for waitresses and dishwashers at a "country hotel." Collins was charged with abducting the girls and was jailed but an accomplice, Tillie Hill, escaped.

In September 1907, William Caruthers' dance hall at 421 Pennsylvania St. was the scene of a double murder and suicide. Edward Mowery, trying to reconcile with ex-lover Jeanette Jones, saw her dancing with a sailor and shot her in the head. The sailor, Jack Ratch grabbed a gun and chased Mowery but also was shot dead by Mowery. The *Sacramento Bee* reported that Mowery ran for about a block but "realizing that flight was useless, placed the muzzle of the weapon in his mouth and blew out his brains."

Six weeks later, a just-discharged sailor named Edmund Curtois, in a room at Caruthers' place with a prostitute named Ella Thompson, shot her twice in the head and then shot himself in the head. He died a few hours later and Thompson, described in a Napa Journal story about the case as a "woman of the half world," died several days later. The murders, suicides and other incidents led to efforts by the Navy and the city of Vallejo, supported by church and temperance groups, to shut down the district. It didn't happen overnight, but Tule Town's days were numbered.

Besides crackdowns by authorities, in 1913 the city started an ambitious project to fill in part of the Napa River that once separated Vallejo from South Vallejo. When the work was completed several years later Pennsylvania Street no longer bordered on the river. Most of the saloons, dance halls and "female boarding" structures were torn down, and by 1919, they had been replaced by apartments, a carpenter shop, auto shop, a lumber company and other non-controversial businesses. One of the original "female boarding" buildings may still be standing at 409 Pennsylvania Street. Its current owner says the structure, now an apartment house, is more than 100 years old.

Vallejo Murder Led to Historic Trial (Dec. 6, 2020)

The trial nearly a century ago of a Vallejo, Calif., thug who killed his city street department boss was no ordinary court proceeding. The case that ended with Martin Colwell going to prison for the rest of his life marked the first, precedent-setting use of bullet "fingerprints" as evidence in American courts.

Colwell's 1926 conviction for gunning down John McCarty was not easy for the prosecution despite strong circumstantial evidence, including Colwell's threats of revenge after McCarty fired him from a street labor gang two days before the shooting. Colwell also was known to be violent and had a lengthy criminal record that resulted in three previous prison terms, one for burglary and two for assaults with a deadly weapon.

But prosecutors, after one deadlocked trial in a Fairfield courtroom, managed in a second trial to convince jurors of Colwell's guilt—with the help of famed criminologist Edward O. Heinrich, their star witness. Heinrich, the so-called "Wizard of Berkeley" and "American Sherlock Holmes," produced microscopic evidence that the bullet fired point-blank into McCarty's chest could only have been fired from Colwell's .38 revolver.

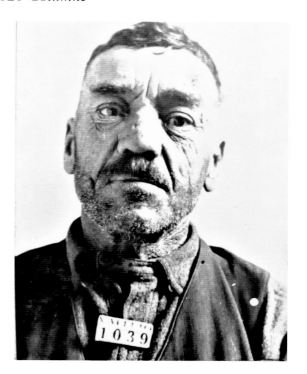

Vallejo thug Martin Colwell was convicted in 1926 of murdering his boss who had fired him from a city labor crew. His trial marked the first use of bullet "fingerprints" in American courts. (*Vallejo Naval and Historical Museum*)

Heinrich reached his conclusion after test-firing a live bullet found in Colwell's pocket, along with several others from a box of ammunition found in the defendant's waterfront ark. Using a stereoscopic microscope, he compared the bullets with the bullet that killed McCarty and found similar rifling scratches on all of them. He then produced photographs of the marks, which he called "bullet fingerprints." Such images had not been seen before in U.S. courts.

Heinrich explained that gun manufacturers, to improve bullet accuracy, used steel bars with cutting edges to make spiral riflings inside gun barrels, and the rifling marks were never identical. The result is a gun barrel "autograph" on any bullet fired from the weapon.

Colwell's second trial began on May 18, 1926, and jurors found him guilty of murder on June 8. Three days later, Superior Court Judge William O'Donnell sentenced him to life in prison. Colwell, 59 when he started his term at San Quentin Prison, was later transferred to Folsom Prison, where he died in 1938. He's buried in the prison cemetery, with a small marker identifying him only as inmate 14237.

On Dec. 19, 1925, McCarty, 40, had just returned from work to his 915 Pennsylvania St. cabin when he heard someone calling him. Shot as he opened his door, McCarty staggered across the street to the Vallejo Ice Co. for help and kept saying, "I fired Colwell." McCarty died in an ambulance taking him to the hospital.

About two hours after the shooting, police arrested Colwell as he headed out of town, walking along the railroad tracks. His .38 revolver, with one chamber empty, was in his pocket along with three bullets. Four shells were gone from the box of shells found in his room. Colwell couldn't account for the missing bullet, insisting he had been drunk the day of the shooting and remembered nothing. Officers also found opium, cocaine and other drugs, describing him as "a walking drug store."

Besides his state prison time, Colwell also had served county jail time. One newspaper account said he had "run amuck" in 1912 while being held at the Solano County jail in Fairfield and was sent to the state hospital in Napa. He escaped from that institution in 1916. Colwell used the aliases John Barry, Joe Kelly and Marty Holleran, but no matter what name he used Colwell wasn't hard to identify. He had tattoos of an eagle, flags, an anchor, girls and stars on his arms and back, and of a full-rigged sailing ship on his chest.

When not behind bars, Colwell, a Massachusetts native, had all sorts of jobs around Vallejo over a span of more than 30 years. Besides his street repair job, he had worked as a printer, fireman and carpenter and in his 20s may have acted in local theater groups. He also had merchant seaman papers and enlisted in the Navy at Mare Island in 1888. He had managed to save some money—and used his savings to retain two prominent Vallejo lawyers, Thomas J. Horan and Arthur Lindauer, a former Solano County district attorney, to fight the charge that he killed McCarty.

During the first trial, Vallejo Police Chief William Stanford testified that Colwell made a jail cell comment that "If I did kill him, it was not me—it was whiskey." But the defense attorneys managed to get a deadlock—seven for conviction, five against— mainly by putting on another criminologist, Chauncey McGovern, to contradict Heinrich's expert testimony.

In the second trial, the defense offered new alibi witnesses and kept trying to discredit Heinrich. But he was better prepared this time. At a juror's request, approved by the judge, Heinrich set up his microscope in the courtroom to demonstrate how he photographed the bullets. One by one, jurors walked up to the microscope and peered into it. He also took additional photos that matched earlier images supporting the prosecution argument that the fatal bullet was fired from Colwell's gun. After closing arguments, jurors deliberated for only an hour and five minutes before returning with their unanimous guilty verdict.

Over the years, there have been references to the trial in articles and books about criminology and forensic firearm examination. They include a March 2008 paper about Heinrich published by the American College of Forensic Examiners. The paper includes details of the precedent-setting Colwell trial and concludes that Heinrich, who died in 1953, "would have enjoyed seeing the procedures he developed or refined nearly a century ago still being used today to make mute evidence speak."

5

2021 Columns

Gen. Vallejo's Son Was Pioneer California Doctor (Jan. 3, 2021)

A son of Gen. Mariano Vallejo had a tough act to follow given his father's status as one of the most important figures in early California history. But Platon Vallejo made his own mark, becoming the first native-born Californian to be commissioned a U.S. Navy officer and to be licensed as a physician in the state.

Studious and observant, Platon also learned to speak English, Spanish, French, Italian and the unwritten Native American language of the Suisuns, a Patwin tribe whose members included "Chief" Solano, his father's trusted ally in protecting Mexican settlers in Northern California.

Besides his decades of medical service mainly in Vallejo, a city named after his father, Dr. Vallejo also wrote, producing a family memoir and a strong defense of California Indians who he said were unfairly labeled by some early-day historians as lazy, dirty, stupid and hostile. Referring to John McGroarty's book California, Its Story and Romance, Vallejo once wrote, "I have seen histories invented by men who would not tell the truth—if they knew it—but preferred to write and tell lies, lies, lies!"

Dr. Vallejo also had no use for a common view that Californios—pre-statehood residents who, like his family, had lived under Spanish and Mexican flags in what became our nation's 31st state in 1850—were insignificant and addicted to leisure in contrast to hard-working Yankees who swarmed into the state during the Gold Rush.

Born on Feb. 5, 1841, in Sonoma, Platon was one of 14 children of Gen. Vallejo and his wife, Dona Francisca Benicia Carrillo. With Gen. Vallejo in charge of Mexican military forces north of San Francisco, the family home was the scene of much activity. As a boy, Platon met military men, explorers, government officials and world travelers. At age five, he witnessed the infamous Bear Flag Revolt, involving a small group of American settlers who rebelled against the Mexican government and proclaimed California an independent republic. Gen. Vallejo tried to negotiate with the settlers when they arrived at his Sonoma home but wound up being jailed for several weeks at Sutter's Fort in Sacramento.

Platon was educated in secondary schools in Benicia, San Francisco and Baltimore, MD. At age 19 he entered Columbia University in New York as a medical student and graduated near the top of his class in 1864. His studies were interrupted temporarily in 1862 when he treated injured Union and Confederate soldiers, many of them wounded

Platon Vallejo, son of Gen. Mariano Vallejo, was the first native-born California physician. (*Vallejo Naval and Historical Museum*)

during the Civil War's bloody Second Battle of Bull Run. His volunteer service in the New York Sanitary Commission Voluntary Surgeons was in the Washington, D.C., area and northern Virginia.

Following his 1864 graduation, Platon joined the Navy as a commissioned officer and served for a year as assistant surgeon on the USS Farallones, a storeship stationed at Mare Island. That was followed by service as a ship surgeon with the Pacific Steamship Company.

On one of his many voyages Platon met Lily Wiley, and they were married in 1867. At that point, he decided to establish a family medical practice in Vallejo, where a brother and two sisters were living. Within a few years the couple had built a home, still standing, at 420 Carolina St. Over the ensuing years, he became a well-known physician and surgeon, with a practice that extended beyond Vallejo to Napa, Marin and Contra Costa counties. He also assisted with surgeries at the Navy hospital on Mare Island.

Dr. Vallejo also was a story-teller who, in the words of one current historian, had "a penchant for testing the limits of credulity." He relied in part on tales heard from family members and from an old Indian named Tomo, who herded sheep for the Vallejos and also was assigned to "herd" Platon when he was a boy. It was Tomo who taught Platon the language of the Suisun—or Suysun, the spelling that Platon preferred.

In a 1914 memoir, Vallejo wrote about various Indian place names, stating that Mount Tamalpais was a corrupted version of Temel-pa, meaning "near the sea" in the Suysun language; and the source of Petaluma's name was pe-talu-ma, three Suysun words that translate as "Oh! Fair land."

As for Sonoma and its "Valley of the Moon" meaning, Vallejo said his father stated the name came from Sano, the Suysun word for moon. But Tomo told him the Suysun word actually was Sono, or nose, and the Indian name Sono-ma honored a great tribal leader from the distant past who had a big nose. "Everyone is welcome to make his choice," Vallejo wrote. "For myself, I like best the moon version, because it fits better with present facts. The nose has long since passed into dust, the moon is ever here."

Historian Lee Fountain, in a well-researched 1991 *Solano Historian* article, said Platon Vallejo "enjoyed a rich and significant life. Born to comparative luxury, reared in a devout and caring family, educated in the classics and medicine to serve his community, he fulfilled his destiny well."

"He saw his world change from a frontier wilderness to a suburban community in the shadow of a growing metropolitan sphere. In this world, he served unstintingly as a surgeon, obstetrician and family doctor. He reared his family of four daughters by himself after his wife's death (in 1885). He was the mainstay for his aging parents; he was quoted by other doctors as never sending a bill for his services."

Dr. Platon Mariano Guadalupe Vallejo died at age 84, on June 1, 1925, at the San Francisco home of his daughter, Francisca Vallejo McGettigan. He was buried in St. Vincent's Cemetery in Vallejo.

Famed Boxer Had Mare Island, Vallejo Ties (Jan. 17, 2021)

Thomas "Sailor Tom" Sharkey, an Irish immigrant who learned to box in the Navy, began his professional stateside boxing career in Vallejo, Calif., in the mid-1890s and advanced to battle the era's best heavyweights. He made a fortune with his fists, but died broke.

Sharkey, born in 1873, left his home in Dundalk, Ireland, at age 12 and had sailed all over the world on merchant ships by the time he left his teens. At 19, he enlisted in the Navy and began boxing in organized bouts aboard the USS *Philadelphia*. In 1893 through mid-1894, when his ship was based in Honolulu, he knocked out a dozen other boxers, including British Navy heavyweight champion Jack Gardner.

By August 1894 the *Philadelphia* was back on the West Coast, tied up at Mare Island Naval Shipyard. Sharkey, touted as the Navy's heavyweight champion, knocked out three more boxers at matches held that month in nearby Vallejo. Tim McGrath, a manager and trainer in San Francisco, heard about Sharkey's exploits but doubted his boxing skills. He figured on making some easy money by arranging a fight with a better-trained heavyweight and betting against the sailor.

McGrath went to Vallejo and met with some of Sharkey's shipmates—who told him they were willing to bet $25,000 without even knowing who Sharkey would fight. Impressed by the sailors' confidence, he asked to see Sharkey. When barrel-chested "Sailor Tom" showed up McGrath realized his betting strategy was flawed. "I chased my fighter right back to San Francisco because I didn't want him to be killed in a fight," he said in a 1929 newspaper interview. Then McGrath, always on the lookout for promising talent, worked out a deal to manage Sharkey, whose Navy enlistment was coming to an end.

Following his first 1894 stateside fights in Vallejo, where he lived for several post-Navy years, Sharkey had 1895 bouts in Vallejo, Colma and San Francisco. They included a Colma fight against "Australian" Billy Smith, who claimed he was the

Famed heavyweight boxer "Sailor Tom" Sharkey began his professional fight career in Vallejo. (*Vallejo Naval and Historical Museum*)

area's best heavyweight. Sharkey knocked him out in seven rounds. Also that year, he KO'd "Sailor" Burke in the third round of a scheduled 10-round match in Vallejo's old Pavilion hall, located at the northwest corner of Georgia and Sutter streets.

Sharkey's standing among professional heavyweights rose sharply in 1896 with a ring victory in San Francisco over Joe Choynski, a formidable, well-regarded boxer. Later that year, Sharkey also fought Bob Fitzsimmons in San Francisco, winning on a controversial below-the-belt foul call against Fitzsimmons by referee and pioneer gunman Wyatt Earp. Sharkey also had bouts that year against greats Jim Corbett and John L. Sullivan. He was on the road, with fights in Chicago, New York, Philadelphia and Denver—well on his way to a great boxing career.

"Sailor Tom," whose motto was "Never give up the ship," never won a title but battled the best in his years in the ring. He scored 37 knockouts in 54 fights and got knocked out only once, by Fitzsimmons in a 1900 bout in New York. Boxing historians have described him as an early version of Rocky Marciano—an aggressive brawler, short, squat, powerful, rough, with great endurance and seemingly impervious to the hardest punches.

Sharkey's biggest battle was an epic 25-round heavyweight title match against Jim Jeffries at Coney Island, N.Y., filmed under hot arc lights on Nov. 3, 1899. Jeffries, the reigning champion, was 6-foot-2, nearly 30 pounds heavier and had a longer reach but the 5-foot-8 Sharkey went the full distance. He lost the decision, leaving the ring after the hour-and-40-minute brawl with two cracked ribs, a cut-up face and a badly swollen left ear—but still on his feet. Jeffries often referred to Sharkey as his toughest opponent.

After ending his professional boxing career in 1904, Sharkey opened a saloon in New York that was one of the city's showplaces. He also invested in real estate, owned a string of racehorses and got involved in an oil company in Louisiana. When he retired he had a $500,000 fortune, which would be worth about $14 million in today's dollars. But by 1916 his investments had failed badly and he was declared bankrupt in federal court, San Francisco.

In the mid-1920s Sharkey and Jeffries toured the country, giving boxing exhibitions in vaudeville shows. Sharkey also got a few character roles in Hollywood movies, worked as a carnival strongman and hired on at various California race tracks. During World War II, he had a job as a civilian guard in San Francisco. During many of his post-boxing years, he lived in San Francisco and often visited friends in Vallejo.

Suffering from heart problems, Sharkey was in and out of the San Francisco City and County Hospital 10 times in 1952 and 1953. Other fighters, promoters, old-time reporters and followers chipped in to pay his expenses.

Sharkey, 79, died in his sleep at the hospital on April 17, 1953—six weeks after his most famous foe, Jim Jeffries, had died. Author Thomas Myler, in his 2017 book, *New York Fight Nights*, said that the ailing Sharkey, when told that Jeffries had passed away, remarked, "It took a long time but I finally beat the bugger in the end." Many more details of Sharkey's life are included in a 2010 book, *I Fought Them All*, by distant relative Moira Sharkey and her husband Greg Lewis.

Sharkey was buried with full military honors in Golden Gate National Cemetery in San Bruno. A Navy color guard gave "Sailor Tom" a final three-volley salute at the gravesite. He was elected to the Ring Boxing Hall of Fame in 1959 and to the International Boxing Hall of Fame in 2003.

Mare Island's Secret Spy Subs (Feb. 28, 2021)

Mare Island Naval Shipyard had a major, top-secret role during the Cold War, refitting submarines as spy ships that slipped undetected into coastal Russian waters and tapped undersea communication cables in risky U.S. efforts to head off Soviet Union military threats.

There was little public awareness of the purpose of the shipyard work and missions of the Mare Island-based spy subs until 1998, two years after the shipyard's closure, with the publication of *Blind Man's Bluff: The Untold Story of American Submarine Espionage*. Since its printing, the book written by Sherry Sontag and Christopher Drew has been a staple for anyone interested in the U.S. Navy's clandestine "silent service" activity.

Mare Island historian Dennis Kelly, writing about the spy submarines in 2015, said that starting in the early 1970s the shipyard was home to what was known as the Ocean Engineering Program, "one of the most highly classified and important programs in the history of the U.S. military." Under the program, Kelly, who was a longtime shipyard employee, said nuclear subs were secretly modified for intelligence-gathering assignments that were successful "until the American traitor Ronald Pelton sold out his country to the Soviets for $35,000 in the early 1980s."

Pelton, a National Security Agency employee for 14 years, was arrested in 1985 after a Russian defector told authorities Pelton had sold the Soviets information on U.S. intelligence efforts, including the code-named "Ivy Bells" submarine spying. Convicted and sentenced to life in prison with possible parole, he was released from federal custody in 2015.

Mare Island work included 1971 modifications to the USS *Halibut* (SSN-587) that included a fake deep-submergence rescue craft mounted on the vessel's deck. Actually it was a decompression chamber that enabled divers to work safely at extreme depths outside the nuclear sub. Their first job following the shipyard modifications was to utilize the chamber 400 feet down in the Sea of Okhotsk while tapping a telephone cable linking two Soviet naval bases.

Capt. James Bradley Jr., director of undersea warfare at the Office of Naval Intelligence, came up with the wiretap plan. As a boy he had seen "Cable Crossing—Do Not Anchor" signs on the Mississippi River, and had a hunch that there would be similar signs along the Russian coast. It took more than a week for the *Halibut*, running at periscope depth, to spot such a sign on a desolate beach and then find and track the five-inch-diameter cable as it ran out to sea from that point. About 40 miles offshore, divers placed a 3-foot-long external device on the cable, and the eavesdropping success resulted in a second *Halibut* voyage in 1972 to place a larger tap. The second device, nearly 20 feet long and weighing about six tons, was designed to monitor many more phone lines and operate for months at a time.

At the start of the first trip, *Halibut* skipper John McNish kept most of his crew in the dark about the cable-tapping plan. But as the sub left on the second run, McNish briefed the men on their mission and the risks they faced. He also told his men that black boxes filled with explosives had been placed at forward, aft and midship locations, wired for self-destruct. If trapped, the sub would not be boarded and the crew would not be taken alive.

The *Halibut* returned to the Okhotsk site in 1974 and 1975, and other submarines, including the Mare Island-based nuclear subs USS *Seawolf* (SSN-575) and USS *Parche*

(SSN-683), followed the same course. The *Parche* placed another large tap close to the first device and both pods remained there until 1982 when the Soviets, alerted to their location by Ronald Pelton's information, fished them out. One of the taps, marked "Property of the United States," wound up in a Moscow museum for several years.

The *Parche* managed to tap another cable in the Barents Sea, resulting in a treasure trove of Soviet voice and data transmissions described by CIA, NSA and Navy officials as "the crown jewels." The sub made four more voyages to the location, and the Barents Sea eavesdropping provided intelligence throughout the Cold War that officially ended in 1991 with the dissolution of the Soviet Union.

By the end of her 30-year, special-operations career, the *Parche* had become the most decorated vessel in the U.S. Navy. The sub's awards included nine Presidential Unit Citations, 10 Navy Unit Commendations and 13 Expeditionary Medals.

Other submarines directly involved in special-ops spying include another Mare Island-based sub, the USS *Richard B. Russell* (SSN-687), and in recent years the USS *Jimmy Carter* (SSN-23), USS *Connecticut* (SSN-22), and a new USS *Seawolf* (SSN-21). Many other Navy subs have had tasks such as providing cover or serving as decoys during secret missions.

While this column focuses on Mare Island Naval Shipyard's role in the Okhotsk and Barents cable-tapping, *Blind Man's Bluff* provides additional details of U.S. Navy spying on the USSR that began in the late 1940s with diesel-electric subs. One of the

Spy submarine USS *Parche* enters San Francisco Bay in 1991, headed for Mare Island Naval Shipyard. (*Vallejo Naval and Historical Museum*)

first attempts ended in disaster in 1949, when a battery fire led to explosions that sank the USS *Cochino* (SS-345) in the Barents Sea. The USS *Tusk* (SS-426) came to the rescue but seven sailors died and dozens were injured. Despite setbacks, the surveillance efforts continued, with the best-known achievements being the listening pods in the 1970s.

"The special fleet of submarines equipped to tap cables made it possible to listen as Soviet naval headquarters detailed day-to-day frustrations, critiqued missions, and reacted to fears of an American nuclear strike," Sontag and Drew wrote in Blind Man's Bluff. "At a point in time when both superpowers could start nuclear war with a push of a button, this was a rare and crucial look at who the adversary really was."

"There was always a huge risk of a destabilizing incident, even the risk that a submarine might spark real battle," the authors added. "But when the Navy and the intelligence agencies weighed the gains against the possibility of a violent response, they relied on one simple fact: the Soviets were sending out their spies as well."

"Perhaps the entire nuclear arms race was insane, but once it existed, spy subs became a crucial part of dealing with that insanity."

Lofty Goals, Bad End for Vallejo Orphans Home (March 28, 2021)

The Good Templars' Home for Orphans, on a hilltop overlooking Vallejo, kept its doors open to children for nearly 50 years. Lofty goals were pursued—until scandals and other issues at the home, combined with a national trend away from orphanages, led to its closure in 1919.

The Order of Good Templars, a temperance society that started in New York in 1851, bought 103 acres of land from A.S. Wood and John Frisbie, Gen. Mariano Vallejo's son-in-law, in 1867 and laid the cornerstone for a three-story mansion in 1869. The home opened on Oct. 1, 1870, and within a year had taken in more than 100 children. Over time, more than 4,500 boys and girls were admitted.

The early years of the orphanage, detailed in a December 1986 *Solano Historian* article, were busy ones, with acquisition of more land and development of a prosperous farm that included livestock, a dairy, trees, vegetable gardens, and wheat and hay fields. A school opened in 1872, and increasing enrollments resulted in a larger schoolhouse being built in 1881.

The home received many donations that helped to cover expenses. Children were assigned various chores, had nondenominational Sunday school lessons and church services, attended community events, and had free admission to a local movie theater. Many were "half-orphans," children who still had one parent or other family but needed to stay at the orphanage temporarily. Their ages ranged from 18 months to 16 years.

An 1899 report stated that children were "all well and happy," management was good and an expected transfer of donated farmland would clear off all debt, leaving the home well in the black. At that point, about 200 children lived there.

But the land transfer was delayed, donations slowed and over the next several years the number of children dropped to just over 100. A state report in 1908 warned that radical changes were needed because the home was more than $15,000 in debt, buildings were dilapidated, sanitary conditions were poor, and oversight by directors was lax.

The Good Templars' Home for Orphans, in what is now the Vista de Vallejo neighborhood, was home to more than 4,500 children over nearly fifty years. (*Vallejo Naval and Historical Museum*)

One change later that year was to name a new superintendent, W. H. Dunning. But in August 1909 Dunning wound up in jail, accused of lewd conduct with about a dozen boys at the home. Two months later, he went to trial, was convicted and sentenced to 30 years in San Quentin Prison. Dunning was paroled in July 1917.

Another scandal developed at the orphanage in September 1914, when the nude body of an eight-year-old boy was found in an attic crawl space. Royd Burney had been missing for 13 days. His body was badly decomposed and a coroner's jury was unable to determine cause of death. John Neylan, chairman of the state Board of Control, said the boy was killed, but investigators were unable to develop enough evidence to file murder charges against anyone. Neylan also said the home's superintendent, Edwin Neale, was incompetent and the orphanage ran the risk of losing state funds unless he was replaced.

Neale resigned under pressure, but remained in the same line of work. In March 1915 he opened the Vallejo Boys' Home and Trade School, on what's now Broadway Street. His small school, whose students included several boys from the orphanage, operated for a few years but by 1920 was no longer listed in the city directory.

The orphanage made front-page news again in March 1919, with the arrest of another superintendent, Fred. G. Anthony, for lewd conduct with girls at the home. Anthony went to trial two months later, was found guilty and sentenced to an indeterminate term in San Quentin.

By mid-year, the orphanage had only 27 children and directors decided to suspend operations, saying the home had outlived its usefulness. But it still was in the news as a result of an appeal filed by Anthony and a split state Supreme Court decision in March 1921 holding that he didn't get a fair trial due to improper statements by Solano County District Attorney Arthur Lindauer.

The high court said the charge against Anthony was one count of lewd and lascivious conduct with a 12-year-old girl but Lindauer brought up other sex crimes that weren't charged. At one point during the trial, justices said Anthony was describing the orphanage buildings and the prosecutor asked why he hadn't mentioned a room where he had raped a nine-year-old girl and a 13-year-old girl. Since the question was tantamount to calling Anthony a rapist, justices said, "we must hold that the misconduct was so prejudicial as to entitle the defendant to a new trial."

The case wound up being dismissed, with Anthony going free in May 1922, after the girl who testified against him in his first trial declined to testify again. She stated in court that she had never heard of Anthony and had no memory of his 12-day trial in 1919. Other witnesses in the 1919 trial couldn't be located.

Initial plans to turn the closed orphanage into an apartment house fell through and it was rented in 1923 to the Vallejo-Mare Island Golf and Country Club. The mansion was torn down after the golf course moved to Blue Rock Springs, and by the mid-1930s fine homes were being built on the old orphanage property.

There are a few traces left of the orphanage, including an underground cistern and rubble from a concrete foundation. In a 2010 *Times-Herald* article by reporter Sarah Rohrs, ex-Mayor Terry Curtola said he often found rocks and rubble from the home in his yard. The former Curtola house was built on the site of the main orphanage building.

At the nearby home of Tom and Gina Snyder, an old mulberry tree in the front yard may be the last vestige of the extensive Orphans' Home farm that included hundreds of fruit and walnut trees. "We are in love with this tree," Gina Snyder said of the mulberry. "It makes us feel part of the heritage of the neighborhood."

Ping Bodie, Vallejo Baseball Great (April 11, 2021)

COVID concerns will keep the Vallejo, Calif., Admirals from playing ball this season. But fans missing local live games can always soak up some hometown baseball history— like stories about Frank "Ping" Bodie, a zany power hitter for an early-day Vallejo team who made it all the way to the New York Yankees.

Bodie joined the Vallejo Giants, an amateur Inter County League team known to most fans as the Vallejos, in 1906 or 1907 and became the team captain. In a July 4, 1908, game against a Napa team, he hit a homer with two runners on base and Vallejo won 3-2. San Francisco Seals manager Danny Long was in the stands and was impressed. He offered Bodie a contract, and two months later "Ping" was playing for the Seals, a Pacific Coast League team—in the minors and on his way to the majors.

In the Seals' 1910 season Bodie hit an astounding 30 home runs—31 if you count an inside-the-park homer. That was triple the combined totals of three Major League home

"Ping" Bodie (left) and Babe Ruth were feared home-run hitters for the New York Yankees. In Bodie's early baseball years, he played for the Vallejo Giants. (*Vallejo Naval and Historical Museum*)

run leaders who had 10 apiece. Not surprisingly, he got a lot of attention from big clubs and was drafted by the Chicago White Sox.

Starting out on the bench in 1911, Bodie went to White Sox owner Charles Comiskey, who had complained about the lack of hitting on the team, and said, "You want some hitting, put me in the lineup." Comiskey complied, and Bodie, a right-hander, delivered with three good seasons. But after a poor fourth season and some clashes with manager Jimmy Callahan in 1915 the stocky 5'8", 195-pound Bodie returned to the Seals.

Bodie, born and raised in San Francisco, was back in familiar territory. During the off-seasons while playing for the White Sox, he had spent winters in Vallejo with his wife, Vallejo native Annie Ayling Bodie. The couple had been married there, in the downtown Methodist Episcopal Church, in 1908. In his 1915 and 1916 seasons with the Seals, he regained his stroke, hitting above .300 and belting 39 home runs.

In 1917, Bodie was back in the big leagues with the Philadelphia Athletics, batting .291 in 148 games. The following year, he was traded to the Yankees, becoming the first of a dozen Italian-Americans, including Joe DiMaggio, from the San Francisco Bay area to play for the Yanks.

Bodie's real name was Francesco Stephano Pezzolo. To avoid racial prejudices, he went by Frank Bodie. His immigrant Italian father had mined for gold in the remote Eastern California town of Bodie before moving to San Francisco. Bodie had two explanations for "Ping". One was that he got the nickname as a child, and the other was that it was the sound of his 52-ounce bat striking a baseball.

Bodie, famed Yankee slugger Babe Ruth's roommate on the road, quickly realized that Ruth missed few opportunities to break curfew and go out on the town. Years later, he said, "I never saw much of him. I roomed with his suitcase." The line was one of many delivered by Bodie when he was clowning around—which was often. While playing for Philadelphia, he once said, "I and the Liberty Bell are the only attractions in Philadelphia." Describing home run hits, he'd say things like "I crashed the old apple" or "I whaled the onion." Variations on his batting skills included bragging about how he could "massacre the apricot," "mace the pill" or "conk the old potato."

In a 1919 spring training stunt in Florida, Bodie defeated an ostrich in a spaghetti-eating contest. The ostrich stopped at 10 or 11 plates of pasta, and Ping downed one more to win. That story lives on in baseball lore—it was recounted only a few days ago by an announcer during a Yankees–Toronto Blue Jays game.

In three full seasons with the Yankees, Bodie batted .256, .278 and .295. But his time with the club, and in the major leagues, ended in 1921 when he played in only 31 games and batted .172. His season was cut short when he fractured his right ankle sliding into home during an exhibition game against the Pittsburgh Pirates. Bodie returned to the minors, playing in San Francisco, Des Moines, Wichita Falls and San Antonio. In 1921 he even returned briefly to the Vallejos, at shortstop. In 1928 at age 40, he put in a final season with the San Francisco Missions, still hitting homers and batting .348. Three years later, Bodie showed up at the Oakland Oaks' spring training in Fresno hoping to play again. But his comeback bid was short-lived and he finally hung up his spikes.

In a total of nine major-league seasons, Bodie's batting average was .275 with 1,011 hits, 43 home runs, 516 RBIs, and 393 runs scored in 1,050 games. His minor league totals were more impressive: a .320 average, with 1,973 hits, 203 homers, 581 RBIs and 990 runs in 1,787 games. Bodie kept a personal "black book" that showed many disagreements with official scorers. In his own scoring of his years in the minors and majors the never-bashful Bodie had a .400 average.

By 1923 he and his wife Annie were living apart, and in 1925 they divorced. She remained in Vallejo with their two children, a son and daughter. Descendants still living in Vallejo include a grandson, Roy Thompson, his daughter Tina Fowler and her son Justin.

After his long baseball career, at infield and outfield positions in the minors and as an outfielder in the majors, Bodie opened a service station and coffee shop near the Seals' stadium. Roy Thompson says his grandfather also worked as an umpire. That included one game where a sarcastic Bodie, fed up with fans criticizing his calls, climbed into the stands and said he'd stay there for the rest of the game because apparently the view of the game was better than what he could see standing behind home plate.

Bodie eventually moved to Southern California where he was an electrician for 32 years on Hollywood movie lots and a bit actor. In his 70s he returned to San Francisco, where he died of lung cancer at age 74 on Dec. 17, 1961. He's buried in Holy Cross Cemetery in Colma.

Vallejo Once Known as "Little Reno" (May 23, 2021)

Starting in the late 1800s and extending until a few years after World War II, Vallejo had so much illegal gambling activity that it became known as "Little Reno." At one point in the 1940s there were more than three dozen card, dice, slot machine and bookie operations, mainly in back rooms of bars, cafes, pool halls and other businesses in the Northern California city.

With the 1864 establishment of a major Navy shipyard on Mare Island, just across the Napa River, Vallejo saw a gradual increase over the years in bars, houses of prostitution and gambling. This column focuses on the gambling.

A Solano County Grand Jury report for 1893 criticized Vallejo authorities for failing to control criminal activity, and the *San Francisco Call* said that led to a crackdown that included suppression of "all gambling games."

The ban helped to slow the illegal games, but didn't stop them. In 1899 the Waldorf saloon, a notorious downtown Vallejo club, was raided and J. T. Murphy and two other men were arrested for playing keno. Murphy appealed his conviction but ultimately lost in a precedent-setting state Supreme Court decision favoring the town's anti-gambling ordinance.

The gambling problems continued in 1900 when Vallejo's new police chief, Bill Stanford, got warrants accusing 31 people of playing craps, poker, keno and other games at the Leader Saloon, another downtown club. The Waldorf also was investigated again, but the *Vallejo Evening Chronicle* reported that Solano County Sheriff George Savage tipped off gamblers at that club and they fled.

More problems, in the downtown's Lower Georgia Street district and also several blocks away in high-crime "Tule Town," on Pennsylvania Street, led to a public vote against gambling in 1912. Police began conducting more raids—but not always with success. A 1913 *Vallejo Daily Times* account described how William Tobin and Charles McCauley, brother of the city's public works commissioner, were arrested for playing poker. The case went to trial, but jurors cleared them after 15 minutes of deliberation. McCauley and Tobin claimed they were playing pinochle, not poker, and $3 that an officer confiscated from their table wasn't betting money.

During World War I Capt. Harry George, the Mare Island Naval Shipyard commandant, insisted Vallejo authorities reduce various forms of gambling that Navy sailors encountered when on liberty. That resulted in a war of words with Police Judge John Browne who accused the Navy of trying to "purify" Vallejo while running their own gambling games in the form of raffles to promote "Liberty Loan" war bonds. Capt. George countered that Browne appeared to be soft on crime and unfit for judicial office.

There were scattered newspaper reports of gambling in Vallejo in the 1920s and 1930s, followed by a dramatic increase in the illegal games with the start of World War II. That paralleled a huge surge in wartime ship-building and repair work on Mare Island.

While more arrests occurred in the early 1940s, a group called the Citizen Committee of 500 complained that gambling establishments "continue to operate with little or no interference." Navy Capt. G. C. Klein, the acting Mare Island commandant, stated that the "unacceptable condition" was causing problems for shipyard workers and sailors who had to be "at their highest productive capacity" during the war. Vallejo Mayor George C. Demmon also demanded a stronger effort to stop the gambling.

The pressure produced results. In a March 1945 report, the *Vallejo News Chronicle* said the police department "announced that the lid is being clamped down on all gambling activities 'of any and all description' in this vicinity. This includes all illegal games of cards, dice, Chinese bean and button games, and even the lowly but profitable pastimes of bingo and punch boards."

More raids of suspected gambling locations were conducted in 1947 and 1948 in the Vallejo area, including one in May 1948 at a Benicia Road chicken ranch that led to arrests of 109 people. Also in 1948, Vallejo Police Chief Earl Dierking was fired and replaced by Jack Stiltz, a reform-minded officer who had been head of the department's vice squad.

Chief Stiltz stepped up enforcement, ordering multiple raids against gambling and other criminal activity in 1949 and 1950, and started getting death threats as a result. His son, Jack Stiltz Jr., says his father avoided an assassination attempt thanks to an informant's tip that he was being targeted.

Gambling was still part of the Lower Georgia scene in the post-WWII years, but local reformers were helped by U.S. Senate hearings into illegal gambling and mob activity. The Special Committee to Investigate Organized Crime in Interstate Commerce, created in 1950 and chaired by Sen. Estes Kefauver, met in 14 major U.S. cities in 15 months, grilling mobsters and amassing reams of material on gangland activities.

The Kefauver Committee's report included details about race wires utilized by bookmakers—and ignored by authorities in many cases. Several Vallejo locations and individuals were listed as clients of Pioneer News Service, a major race wire. The California Public Utilities Commission also held lengthy hearings into the wire network.

The California Legislature followed up with two new laws aimed at driving slot machines out of the state. Gov. Earl Warren signed the new laws on April 26, 1950, saying that they and the PUC action against the race wires were "perhaps the two things which can be made to do the most to cut off the profits of the underworld."

Congress then approved a law, signed Jan. 2, 1951, by President Truman, prohibiting transportation of gambling devices across state lines. The law also banned slot machines on land under federal jurisdiction. Mare Island Naval Shipyard and other military bases

The Rex Club (center) was one of many businesses in Vallejo's Lower Georgia Street sailor district that ran illegal gambling operations. (*Thomas W. Atkinson, Jr., photo*)

immediately removed and destroyed the "one-armed bandits" that had been in clubs for officers and non-coms.

Some gambling activity continued for many years in the Vallejo area, particularly in the Filipino community, but the heyday was over. Operators of some Lower Georgia joints, including the Rex Club, Dopey Norman's and C & S Sportland, decided it was time to move on and went to Nevada where gambling was legal. The Lower Georgia Street district continued in a downward slide and by 1970 the entire area was bulldozed into history as part of a major downtown redevelopment project.

Controversial South Vallejo Flour Mill Has Long History (June 20, 2021)

It's hard to say what the future holds for an old waterfront mill in South Vallejo, in light of criminal proceedings against its top two executives, Alan Varela and William Gilmartin. But there's no guesswork involved when you look at its long history: Over time, what started out as a small operation run by Abraham Starr 152 years ago became one of the most important flour mills in California. The site now has historic landmark status, at both the state and local level.

Varela and Gilmartin were implicated in a probe into bribes paid to Mohammed Nuru while he was San Francisco's public works director. They recently pleaded guilty to wire fraud charges that could lead to maximum 20-year prison terms and stiff fines. Their Sperry Mill Group LLC leases most of the old mill from the City of Vallejo, and it remains to be seen whether the city wants to keep that lease arrangement. One alternative would be to follow San Francisco's lead and cut off any business dealings with the two men. Other individuals and entities, including the nearby California State University Maritime Academy, have expressed interest in some form of involvement with the mill site.

The mill's history dates to 1869 when Starr, a '49er who turned from gold-mining to milling, convinced the Southern Pacific Railroad to extend tracks to the south end of the Mare Island Strait. He built a dock, warehouse and mill that could produce about 250 barrels of flour a day, figuring the location was ideal because of its easy access to San Francisco Bay and the Pacific Ocean, as well as to the San Joaquin Delta and inland California. The railroad extension linked the mill to the newly completed transcontinental railroad which, in turn, connected the mill to all points along that route, from the Pacific to the Atlantic. The flour was first distributed into Northern California and, as production increased, was shipped to Europe, Central America, Hawaii, Australia, China and Japan on clipper ships.

Starr, in poor health and burdened by financial and family problems, died in 1894 at age 64. The Stockton-based Sperry Flour Co., founded in 1852 by another miner-turned-miller, Austin Sperry, and expanded in an 1892 merger with several other mills, bought the South Vallejo mill and closed it. The following year, the Port Costa Flour Co., owned by George Washington McNear, the so-called "wheat king of California," first leased and then bought the mill and increased production to more than 2,000 barrels a day.

The rival Sperry Flour Co. continued to add mills but in the disastrous 1906 earthquake its San Francisco plant was totally destroyed. In need of more production capacity, Sperry decided in 1910 to buy back the South Vallejo mill that it had sold to

An early drawing of the original 1869 Starr Mill on the South Vallejo side of the Mare Island Strait. The flour mill, which expanded and changed owners over the years, operated until 2004. (*Vallejo Naval and Historical Museum*)

McNear 15 years earlier and started a major expansion. There were setbacks, including an Aug. 29, 1916, fire caused by defective wiring that burned down a mammoth grain warehouse. Also destroyed were about 125,000 sacks of flour, 13 railroad box cars and five vehicles. The fire was described at the time as the worst in Vallejo history. But the mill's expansion and productivity continued, fueled by high demand from America's European allies for imported flour during World War I. Employment at the mill nearly tripled, to more than 360 workers. The expansion included construction of an eight-story mill and warehouse, huge grain elevator, storage bins, a garage and two-story administration building, designed by prominent civil engineer Maurice Couchot.

The 1920s brought big changes to the Sperry Flour Co. The industry had expanded during WW1, but demand for flour decreased in post-war years and in 1924 the South Vallejo mill shut down again. James Bell and Harry Bullis, of the newly formed General Mills Corp. in Minneapolis, saw opportunity during the post-war consolidation period, and in May 1929 acquired Sperry Flour Co. as a subsidiary. The mill continued to operate, although another big fire in 1934 burned down a large bulk storage building and destroyed 6,000 tons of wheat, corn, barley and oats.

World War II marked another milestone for the mill as its production continued to increase. Mare Island Naval Shipyard also utilized the mill for ship-docking, among other things, as part of a cross-river expansion that was needed due to the huge increase in shipyard activity. As the end of the war neared, General Mills executives drafted plans to avoid another post-war slump by developing a greater variety of products and operating more efficiently. They also decided to replace the name "Sperry Flour" with "General Mills" on the grain silos. A new feed warehouse was completed in 1947 and was connected by a conveyor shed to the old Starr Mill—but both were destroyed by a third major fire in 1957. Today, part of the dock and piles on which the mill and warehouse once stood are all that remain of the original Starr mill.

Tom Bartee, a former manager at the mill, says that in the 1950s the plant employed about 250 people and produced 800,000 pounds of flour daily. Production remained at that level in the 1960s, with the mill shipping its products by truck and rail every day, but employment had dropped to 150. By the early 1990s plant upgrades raised production to 1.5 million pounds daily although employment was down to about 90. Finally, in early 2004 the number of mill workers had dropped to 60 and abrupt layoffs cut that number to about 40. The following September, General Mills announced it was shutting down the plant and selling the property. The last day on the job for remaining workers was Dec. 3, 2004.

Vallejo Went Wild on V-J Day (Aug. 15, 2021)

This Aug. 14–15 weekend marks the 76th anniversary of the surrender of Japan, effectively ending World War II. Reacting to the Aug. 14, 1945, announcement of the surrender, thousands of jubilant people jammed into downtown Vallejo for the biggest celebration the Navy shipyard town had ever seen.

"Vallejo Goes Wild as War Ends—Streets Overrun With Gay Revelers," the next morning's *Vallejo Times-Herald* banner headline declared. The front-page story stated, "Screaming sirens and blasting horns heralded President Truman's declaration of peace, and throngs hysterical with joy paraded through the downtown streets."

Vallejoans were ready for peace. During the war years, 228 soldiers, sailors, aviators and Marines from their town had died. Residents were proud of Mare Island Naval Shipyard's amazing record of ship construction and repair, but had to cope with a huge wartime population increase, rationing and a round-the-clock shipyard work regimen.

Times-Herald staff photographer Bill Platt captured the celebrating with photos including one of sailors kissing and hugging women in front of the Georgian Hotel, in Vallejo's notorious Lower Georgia Street district—his own version of an iconic shot, taken the same day, of a sailor passionately kissing a nurse in New York City's Times Square. The local photo caption read, "Very few girls escaped being kissed during the four hours following the announcement as enthusiastic servicemen celebrated the war's end. Those who did escape were either very uncooperative or very fleet of foot."

Other photos by Platt showed people blowing horns, tossing confetti and passing around bottles of liquor on the street, smiling and waving workers getting off a ferryboat that had just brought them across Mare Island Strait from the shipyard to the foot of Georgia Street, and a large crowd milling around on Marin Street in the center of town.

"The announcement of the end of World War II was made over Mare Island's public address system at 4:01 p.m. on Tuesday, Aug. 14, 1945. Whistles, bells, sirens and horns broke out in a tumultuous celebration," author Arnold Lott wrote in *A Long Line*

The Vallejo *Times-Herald* headline declared the town went wild following the August 14, 1945, announcement that Japan had surrendered, effectively ending World War II. (*Vallejo Naval and Historical Museum*)

of Ships, his 1954 book packed with extensive details of Mare Island history up to that point. "The swing-shift crew, just arriving for work, heard that the President had declared a two-day holiday; they immediately wheeled about and headed home again, along with everyone else, in the granddaddy of all traffic jams."

Japan's unconditional surrender followed the U.S. decision to drop atomic bombs on Hiroshima on Aug. 6 and on Nagasaki on Aug. 9. Both Aug. 14 and Aug. 15 became known as Victory Over Japan Day, or simply V-J Day, and eventually Sept. 2 was designated as V-J Day in America. That marked the day in 1945, when Japan's formal surrender took place aboard the USS *Missouri* in Tokyo Bay.

A story in the Aug. 15, 1945, *Vallejo News-Chronicle* stated that the city "awakened to the first day of peace today with a morning-after feeling that combined the effects of a Fourth of July celebration, a New Year's Eve jamboree, a lodge clambake and a bartender's convention."

Thirty people were treated for minor injuries and 17 were arrested "on disturbance charges," the newspaper stated. A few store windows were broken, including one at a liquor store where seven cases of port wine were stolen.

About 75 laughing men and women climbed onto a fire truck responding to a downtown call and wouldn't get off until the truck returned to a nearby fire station. At least a dozen false alarms were called in; and fire-fighters also had to douse many "Victory bonfires" set on downtown streets. Also, Police Officer Edward "Robbie" Robinson, attempting to direct traffic, suffered a broken leg when hit by a drunken driver.

The news reports stated that the president's announcement, detailed in newspaper "extras" that were immediately sold out, "came just as thousands of Mare Island workers were changing shifts and the homecoming war workers joined with crowds of shoppers and servicemen who seemed to literally pour into the Georgia-Marin central area."

"Almost immediately after peace was announced, all local stores and bars closed their doors. A great number of eating-houses also shut their doors to celebrate the good news. A liquor shortage was not noticeable in the streets of Vallejo in spite of the tavern shutdown. V-J Day bottles were much in evidence and sailors and girls shared them in impromptu toasts along the sidewalks."

"At the moment victory was officially announced the city hall siren started a blast that was joined by other local sirens, police equipment and private motorists' horns. The serpentine parade of cars with radios and horns in full blast continued through the city streets for many hours. Streets in the center of town were overrun by the revelers, who hailed passing motorists and crowded on running boards and fenders."

But the celebrating in Vallejo was mild compared with nearby San Francisco, where violence left 11 people dead and nearly a thousand injured. San Francisco Police Chief Charles Dulles said a mob on the busiest section of Market Street broke "every window within three blocks." The violence and looting led to orders that all military personnel get off the streets and return to their duty stations. Those orders, rescinded after 24 hours, covered San Francisco and any areas within 100 miles of the city—including Vallejo.

Within four days after VJ Day, about 1,000 Mare Island workers quit, some without bothering to collect their pay. On one ship, several workers tossed their tool boxes into the Napa River. "Won't them any more," one of the workers explained. Within a month, the shipyard went back to a 5-day work week, the graveyard shift was ended and nearly 7,000 employees had been let go.

Production on Mare Island in support of the war effort was huge. Workers built 386 ships, including four submarine tenders, 17 submarines, 31 destroyer escorts, 33 small craft of various types, and 301 landing craft. From 1940 through 1945, the yard also repaired a total of 1,227 ships. Patriotism ran high. Mare Island's military and civilian workforce raised nearly $76 million in war bonds.

By mid-1946, the WW2 shipyard workforce that had swelled to more than 40,000 dropped back to where it was in 1940, about 12,000 employees. While shipyard hiring never again came anywhere near its WWII level, Mare Island remained active until it was decommissioned on April Fools' Day, 1996.

COVID, Spanish Flu Deaths in Solano (Sept. 26, 2021)

Recent news reports describe Solano County as lagging behind in the San Francisco Bay area in responding to the lethal COVID-19 pandemic. Tragically, the county's coronavirus-related death toll has topped 300 and is drawing closer to its total of 341 Spanish Flu deaths a century ago.

Old state records and news accounts show a strong effort within Solano County to control the 1918–20 Spanish Flu pandemic. Given medical advances, demographic changes, politics and other factors, it's a bit of a stretch to compare that effort with today's county-wide response to COVID-19. Even so, the recent news stories and current statistics are telling.

Solano's COVID-19 full vaccination rate, 54.4 percent, is the lowest of the nine Bay Area counties. It also has a high daily infection rate and a hospitalization rate two to three times higher than that of other local counties. Solano also trailed several other counties last year in imposing stay-home orders, waiting until the state required it.

Last week, county supervisors voted 3-2 not to mandate COVID-19 vaccinations or protective masks for county employees. However, they're not objecting to mask requirements adopted by cities within the county. Vallejo and Benicia, with higher-than-average vaccination rates, require most people to wear masks indoors in public buildings.

What happened a century ago when the Spanish Flu was first seen in this area? The influenza hit this area in waves, starting in late September 1918 when the first case was reported on Mare Island Naval Shipyard. Research by Capt. Thomas Snyder, MC, USNR (Ret.) shows the Navy was alerted in advance but there was inadequate planning in Vallejo. The town was overcrowded due to a large wartime increase in shipyard workers, and that made spread of the contagion inevitable.

The Navy set up a tent city to serve as an annex to the Naval Hospital, banned large gatherings and allowed no liberty for sailors in Vallejo. The Vallejo City Council followed up with orders to shut down theaters, dance halls, libraries, schools, churches and other "public assembly" sites. Face masks were mandated and two emergency hospitals opened in town, in addition to the small existing hospital.

A 1918 photo shows members of the William Topley family in front of their Vallejo home during the Spanish Flu epidemic. (*Vallejo Naval and Historical Museum*)

The health crisis seemed to abate by late 1918, but another influenza wave hit in January 1919. Public assembly sites again closed, face masks were again required, and stiff penalties were assessed for people—labeled "dangerous slackers" by the Red Cross—who refused to wear the masks.

The *Vallejo Evening Chronicle* reported that a local judge's desk was "piled high with $5 fines" as he politely listened to the stories of violators "and then just as politely ordered: $5 please, next case!" Those $5 fines were the equivalent of about $100 today.

A third wave of Spanish Flu cases hit the area in early 1920, resulting in a ban on indoor public meetings and other restrictions. But by mid-February the restrictions were lifted. The most devastating phase of the pandemic was over.

Among the Solano County victims were Marian Turner, a nurse in charge of an influenza ward on Mare Island; prominent farmers Morris Buck of Vacaville and Dan O'Connell of Benicia; well-known Vallejo businessman Adolph Widenmann; three daughters and one son of the Bert Evins family, Dixon farmers; Vallejo banker B. F. Griffin and his daughter-in-law, Mrs. Roscoe Griffin; and a Navy doctor, Lt. Edward McColl.

According to old California Board of Health reports, the Spanish flu killed 341 people in Solano County between 1918 and 1920. Another 169 deaths in the same period were caused by pneumonia, and many probably were linked to the deadly influenza. Three-quarters of all known victims were from Vallejo and Mare Island while the rest were from small towns. The county's population then was about 40,000, compared with a current total of just over 450,000.

Solano County's death toll was dwarfed by the 3,829 influenza deaths from 1918 to 1920 in San Francisco. However, there were no deaths of Navy sailors stationed on nearby Yerba Buena Island due to orders that nobody was to leave unless reassigned elsewhere and that any visitors stay 10 feet away from those based on the island.

The U.S. death total from the Spanish Flu was about 675,000. Globally, there were at least 50 million victims. Before COVID-19, the flu was universally considered the worst pandemic disease in human history. In the U.S., the coronavirus death total is now equal to the Spanish Flu total, and its global total is nearing 5 million.

The ebbing of COVID-19 could happen if the virus progressively weakens as it mutates and peoples' immune systems learn to attack it. A recent Associated Press story says something similar happened with the H1N1 virus, the culprit in the Spanish Flu pandemic. It encountered too many people who were immune, and it also weakened through mutation. H1N1 still circulates today, but immunity through infection and vaccination has triumphed.

No vaccine existed at the time to slow the spread of the Spanish flu—wrongly named because it first received widespread news coverage in Spain. Also, there were no antibiotics to treat secondary bacterial infections. There have been major advances in scientific knowledge since then, but there also is a failure to take maximum advantage of vaccines that are now available.

An estimated 39 percent of the world population may be fully vaccinated, based on the number of vaccine doses administered. The full vaccination total in the U.S., including adults and children, is 55 percent, while state percentage rates range from the high 60s in Vermont, Connecticut, Maine and Massachusetts to the low 40s in Idaho, West Virginia, Alabama and Mississippi. California's rate is about 58 percent.

Compared with Solano County's 54.4 percent rate for full vaccinations, the eight other San Francisco Bay area counties have percentage rates ranging from the high 60s to the high 70s. Marin County is highest at about 77 percent.

Old Shipyard Flagpole is Unsafe (Oct. 10, 2021)

An important flagpole has stood at the same central location on the former Mare Island Naval Shipyard since the shipyard, just north of San Francisco, was established in 1854. The current flagpole may not be the original one, but is so old and in such bad shape that it's now considered a safety hazard.

With its distinctive crows-nest that makes it look like a ship's mast, the historic, 60-foot-tall flagpole is considered the most prominent feature in Alden Park, on the south side of the shipyard's main administration building. Due to its deteriorated condition, the pole must be repaired or, as a last resort, replaced. To cut it down and have no flagpole in the park is not an option.

Vallejo, just across Mare Island Strait, now controls the island. The city's planning, public works and legal departments are all involved in determining what happens next. A city Architectural Heritage and Landmarks Commission review also is expected. For now, yellow safety tape keeps people from getting too close to the flagpole.

"We are reaching out to both an engineering consultant and an Architectural Historian to explore the best way to preserve the flagpole," city Planning Director Christina Ratcliffe said in response to an e-mail inquiry. "We will be coming before the AHLC as soon as we have more information on that."

The first flagpole was put in place soon after Navy Commander David Farragut took charge of the shipyard on Sept. 16, 1854. Two days later, Farragut initiated the flagpole

A flagpole stood at the same spot on the former Mare Island Naval Shipyard since 1854. The current flagpole has deteriorated and is unsafe. (*Rick Mariani photo*)

construction, hiring a few men to build a foundation. The pole went up on Oct. 2, and the American flag was raised the next day, in a brief ceremony witnessed by the entire shipyard force of a dozen workers. The USS *Warren*, which on Sept. 18 became the first Navy ship to arrive at Mare Island, fired a 13-gun salute.

In *A Long Line of Ships*, Arnold Lott's book detailing Mare Island's history, Lott wrote that the arrival of the *Warren* had "lent a military atmosphere to the scene." But Lott wrote that Farragut, who ran off several squatters on the day he took over, wanted the Stars and Stripes waving from flagpole as soon as possible to clearly "indicate government ownership of the island."

The pole became what's described in a 2014 report on Alden Park as "the central organizing element" for the park as well as for nearby buildings. When the commandant's residence was built near the park in 1855 its front door was deliberately aligned with the flagpole. When a permanent administration building was constructed in 1870, its entry also was aligned with the flagpole. A similar lining-up occurred when the bandstand was built in 1895 on the south side of the pole, and when other park features were added over the years.

The Alden Park report also says that the flagpole is a character-defining feature for the park, and under federal Interior Secretary standards shouldn't be removed. Any deteriorated features "will be repaired rather than replaced," those standards state. And if the deterioration is beyond repair, its replacement has to be as close a match as possible, "in design, color, texture and, where possible, materials."

Concern over the flagpole is nothing new. The issue came up four years ago and Roland Rojas, the city's assistant maintenance superintendent at the time, said the pole needed to be inspected by an engineer to assess its condition and get a cost estimate for restoration. It's not clear whether the inspection ever occurred. In any case, no repair work was done.

Preliminary work by a city crew in 2017 included drilling four small test holes around the base of the flagpole. The base is a foot in diameter, and Rojas reported that the drills went through only an inch-and-a-half of solid wood before encountering rot, caused by moisture in the earth below the pole. He also obtained information on use of a penetrating epoxy to stop the rot. That's a common technique used in wood boat repairs, and in some cases can allow for repairs without completely dismantling whatever is being worked on. The epoxy could be combined with an iron base for added strength.

Rojas stated in 2017 that he was thinking of cutting the pole at its base, removing several feet of rotted wood at the lower end and having epoxy applied to the rest of the pole, which would then be set in the existing concrete foundation. The four guy wires that have been used for decades to stabilize the flagpole would have to be shortened, and Rojas said that would leave most of the pole still in place.

Once the city comes up with a plan for restoring or replacing the flagpole, that plan will be submitted to the Architectural Heritage and Landmarks Commission, which will conduct a public hearing to review and take public comment on the proposal.

Jim Kern, executive director of the Vallejo Naval and Historical Museum, hopes the flagpole can be restored. But even if it has to be replaced, he says that's far better than no flagpole at all.

"Alden Park and the surrounding historic buildings are really the heart and soul of Mare Island. It would be a shame to no longer fly the American flag there after it's flown there continuously for nearly 170 years," Kern adds. "We fly the flag in front of City Hall, the Police Department, and all of our fire stations, so why not there too?"

Epilogue

There is no end to interesting stories about Vallejo, the former Mare Island Naval Shipyard and other communities in Solano County. We are fortunate to live in a community where many local events had repercussions that went well beyond the boundaries of Solano County. Vallejo's namesake, Mariano Vallejo, was one of Mexico's most prominent pre-U.S. statehood leaders in California, and our city is on land once part of his vast holdings. The cities of Vallejo and Benicia were early-day capital cities of California. Mare Island Naval Shipyard's long existence across the Napa River resulted in everything from a wild night life for sailors and shipyard workers on Vallejo's Lower Georgia Street bar district to Navy ship and submarine construction and top-secret spy projects vital to our national security. History-making court proceedings occurred here. Individuals on their respective paths to fame or infamy spent time here, including the controversial duchess of Windsor, ruthless gangster George "Baby Face" Nelson, WWII fighter pilot and hero Grant Mahony, author Ernest Gaines, actor Boris Karloff and others. The future is uncertain, but knowing about our past could help shape that future. As philosopher George Santayana said in the early 1900s, "Those who cannot remember the past are condemned to repeat it."

Bibliography

Allen, R. L., *The Port Chicago Mutiny* (New York, Amistad Press, 1993)

Burrough, B., *Public Enemies* (New York, Penguin Books, 2004)

California Board of Health annual reports, 1918–20.

Gaudet, M. (ed.), *Ernest J. Gaines: Conversations* (Jackson, MS, University of Mississippi Press, 2019)

Grant, E., *Report of Vice Investigation at Vallejo and Benicia and Vicinity in Solano County, California* (College Park, National Archives, 1917)

Guttridge, L. F., *Mutiny: A History of Naval Insurrection* (Annapolis, Naval Institute Press, 2006)

Hubbard, H. D., *Vallejo* (Boston, Meador Publishing, 1941)

Johnson, B., *Report on Conditions Surrounding the Naval Station at Mare Island, California* (College Park, National Archives, 1917)

Kern, J. E., *Images of America: Vallejo* (Charleston, Arcadia Publishing, 2004)

Leach, F. A., *Recollections of a Newspaperman: A Record of Life and Events in California* (San Francisco, Samuel Levinson, 1917)

Lemmon, S. and Wichels, E. D., *Sidewheelers to Nuclear Power* (Annapolis, Leeward Publications, 1977)

Lott, A. S., *A Long Line of Ships* (Annapolis, United States Naval Institute, 1954)

MacGregor, M. J., *Integration of the Armed Forces, 1940–1965* (Washington, D. C., Center of Military History, 1981)

McGriff-Payne, S., *Images of America: African Americans in Vallejo* (Charleston, Arcadia Publishing, 2012)

Moore, W. H., *The Kefauver Committee and the Politics of Crime* (Columbia, University of Missouri Press, 1974)

Nickel, S. and Helmer, W. J., *Baby Face Nelson: Portrait of a Public Enemy* (Nashville, Cumberland House Publishing, 2002)

Okrent, D., *Last Call: The Rise and Fall of Prohibition* (New York, Scribner, 2010)

Oxford, J., *The Capital That Couldn't Stay Put* (San Diego, June Oxford, 1983)

Ramsey, Jr., W. R., *Reports of Special Agent W.R. Ramsey Jr.*, Jan. 22, 1935 and May 10, 1934 (San Francisco, FBI reports produced in the trial of individuals charged with harboring Baby Face Nelson)

Riley, B., *Lower Georgia Street: California's Forgotten Barbary Coast* (Charleston, Fonthill Media LLC and Arcadia Publishing, 2017)

Rosenus, A., *General Vallejo and the Advent of the Americans* (Berkeley, Heyday Books, 1995)

Sheinkin, S., *The Port Chicago 50: Disaster, Mutiny, and the Fight for Civil Rights* (New York, Roaring Brook Press, 2014)

Sides, H., *In the Kingdom of Ice: The Grand and Terrible Polar Voyage of the USS Jeannette* (Doubleday, 2014)

Solano Historian, various issues (Vallejo, Solano County Historical Society)

Sontag, S. and Drew, C., *Blind Man's Bluff: The Untold Story of American Submarine Espionage* (PublicAffairs, 1998)

Truman, H. S, Executive Order 9981 and related documents (Independence, Harry S. Truman Library & Museum)

U.S. Senate Special Committee to Investigate Organized Crime in Interstate Commerce, Hearing Reports, Part 2, June 22–23, June 28, July 6–7, Aug. 16, 1950 (Washington, D.C., U.S. Government Printing Office)

Vallejo newspaper articles and history columns and related materials on Vallejo from other U.S. newspapers, the Associated Press and United Press International

Vallejo Naval and Historical Museum files and Mare Island Museum files

Van Tilburg, H., *A Civil War Gunboat in Pacific Waters: Life on Board USS Saginaw* (University Press of Florida, 2010)

Watterson, R. K., *Whips to Walls: Naval Discipline from Flogging to Progressive Era Reform at Portsmouth Prison* (Annapolis, Naval Institute Press, 2014)